# BRABHAM CARS

ISBN 1 84155 619 X

www.cppress.co.uk

# CONTENTS

# BRABHAM BT26A FORD SPECIFICATIONS

**ENGINE**

Cosworth - Ford DFV

**BORE AND STROKE**

85.6mm x 64.8mm

**CAPACITY**

2995cc

**GEARBOX**

Hewland DG300

**HALF SHAFTS**

Rotaflex couplings, double universals

**FRONT AND REAR SUSPENSION**

Double wishbones outboard springs

**WHEELBASE**

95 inches

**FRONT TRACK**

56 inches

**REAR TRACK**

61.5 inches

# REPCO BRABHAM 1967
# ESSENTIAL SPECIFICATIONS

**ENGINE**

Repco V8

**BORE AND STROKE**

3.5 inches x 2.55 inches

**CAPACITY**

2996cc

**MAXIMUM POWER**

326 at 8200

**GEARBOX**

Hewland DG

**CHASSIS**

MRD Multitubular

**SUSPENSION**

**Front:** Unequal length double wishbones, outboard coil spring / damper units

**Rear:** Unequal length double wishbones, outboard coil spring / damper units

**FRONT TRACK**

53 inches

**REAR TRACK**

55.5 inches

**WHEELBASE**

93.5 inches

# BRABHAM BT33 FORD SPECIFICATIONS

**ENGINE**

Cosworth - Ford DFV

**BORE AND STROKE**

85.6mm x 64.8mm

**COMPRESSION**

11:1

**MAXIMUM POWER**

430 @ 10,000

**GEARBOX**

Hewland DG300

**CHASSIS**

Brabham aluminium alloy monocoque

**SUSPENSION**

**Front:** Double wishbones inboard springs

**Rear:** Double wishbones outboard springs

**WHEELBASE**

95 inches

**FRONT TRACK**

58.25 inches

**REAR TRACK**

61.25 inches

# BRABHAM BT34
# FORD SPECIFICATIONS

**ENGINE**

Cosworth - Ford DFV

**BORE AND STROKE**

85.6mm x 64.8mm

**CAPACITY**

2993cc

**MAXIMUM POWER**

440 @ 10,000

**CHASSIS**

Brabham aluminium alloy monocoque

**SUSPENSION**

**Front:** Double wishbones outboard springs

**Rear:** Lower wishbones top links, radius rods, outboard springs

**WHEELBASE**

95 inches

**FRONT TRACK**

63 inches

**REAR TRACK**

64 inches

# BRABHAM BT37
# FORD SPECIFICATIONS

**ENGINE**

Cosworth - Ford DFV

**BORE AND STROKE**

85.6mm x 64.8mm

**CAPACITY**

2993cc

**COMPRESSION RATIO**

11 : 1

**MAXIMUM POWER**

450bhp @ 10,000

**GEARBOX**

Hewland FG400 / FL400

**SUSPENSION**

**Front:** Double wishbones outboard springs

**Rear:** Parallel lower links, single top links, twin radius rods, outboard springs

**WHEELBASE**

96 inches

**FRONT TRACK**

60.5 inches

**REAR TRACK**

61 inches

# BRABHAM BT39 WESTLAKE SPECIFICATIONS

### ENGINE

Weslake - Ford 190

### BORE AND STROKE

75mm x 56.46mm

### CAPACITY

2995cc

### COMPRESSION RATIO

11.5 : 1

### MAXIMUM POWER

455bhp @ 10,500

### GEARBOX

Hewland FG400

### SUSPENSION

**Front:** Double wishbones outboard springs

**Rear:** Parallel lower links, single top links, twin radius rods, outboard springs

### WHEELBASE

100 inches

### FRONT TRACK

56 inches

### REAR TRACK

61 inches

# BRABHAM BT42
# FORD SPECIFICATIONS

**ENGINE**

Cosworth - Ford DFV

**BORE AND STROKE**

85.6mm x 64.8mm

**CAPACITY**

2993cc

**MAXIMUM POWER**

460bhp @ 10,250 rpm

**GEARBOX**

Hewland FG400

**SUSPENSION**

**Front:** Double wishbones outboard springs

**Rear:** Parallel lower links, single top links, twin radius rods, outboard springs

**WHEELBASE**

94 inches

**FRONT TRACK**

57.5 inches

**REAR TRACK**

57 inches

# BRABHAM BT44
# FORD SPECIFICATIONS

**ENGINE**

Cosworth - Ford DFV

**BORE AND STROKE**

85.6mm x 64.8mm

**CAPACITY**

2993cc

**COMPRESSION RATIO**

11 : 1

**MAXIMUM POWER**

460bhp @ 10,250 rpm

**GEARBOX**

Hewland FG400

**SUSPENSION**

**Front:** Double wishbones outboard springs

**Rear:** Parallel lower links, single top links, twin radius rods, outboard springs

**WHEELBASE**

95 inches

**FRONT TRACK**

56.5 inches

**REAR TRACK**

60 inches

# Brabhams dominate the Tasman series

The Brabham 2.5 litre Intercontinental car proved invincible in the Australian part of the Formula Tasman series, Jack himself winning three of the four events and Graham Hill winning the fourth in a privately-entered Brabham. Bruce McLaren and his Cooper team went to Australia full of hope, after dominating the New Zealand Series, but enjoyed no luck and finally suffered the loss of Timmy Mayer while practising for the Longford meeting. McLaren had collected enough points in New Zealand to win the Championship.

Of the local drivers, Frank Matich proved the biggest threat to ex-World Champions, leading them on occasions by stints of fiery and impetuous driving which tested the reliablity of his cars; he finished one race only.

## Australian Grand Prix

The series opened with the major event, held this year at the Sandown Park circuit near Melbourne. It was in this event last year that Jack Brabham scored his first win in his own car, at Sydney, but this year he had to beat the Cooper bogey that got the better of him each time in New Zealand. He and McLaren were fastest in practice, followed by Matich in his Total-sponsored new Brabham which was faster than Denis Hulme's Brabham, a year-old car.

Of the 26 starters for the 63 lap, 121-mile event, 15 cars were equipped with the 2½ litre power units and the remainder were using 1½ litre engines, all Ford-based, competing for the Australian National Championship.

The radiator on McLaren's car was damaged in the pits only half an hour before the start, needing to be changed very quickly so it was a flustered New Zealander who hurried to his place in the front row of the grid. A spirited take-off took him into the lead before the first corner with Matich in hot pursuit, but behind them Lex Davison spun and put the rest of the field into disarray. Everyone avoided everyone and Brabham, who almost finished his race there and then, took advantage of the melee to secure third place. Mayer moved up behind him, harried by Bib Stillwell's Brabham.

Jack very soon closed on Matich and passed him, and Frank broke his gearbox a couple of laps later forcing his retirement. Brabham was keeping McLaren's Cooper well in view, and after 25 laps had overtaken this adversary. The New Zealander regained the lead next time round and for the next 12 laps the big crowd was treated to some really close-quarter and exciting racing, until McLaren's engine blew up spectacularly in front of the pits. This left Jack with a full half-minute lead over Mayer, who had managed to pull away from Stillwell, making the leader-board fairly predictable for the time being.

Behind them, Denny Hulme was providing much interest in his Brabham, having got to grips with John Youl's Cooper, and for a while attention was focussed upon them and not on Brabham, who was by now taking things very easily, allowing Stillwell to get within 12 seconds by the finish. Mayer dropped his second place with only six laps to go when fuel starvation was cutting his motor, and he had to slow down and watch both Stillwell and Youl go past in close company. Hulme, too, was left behind when he made a pit-stop to investigate overheating troubles, putting him three laps in arrears at the end.

**RESULTS**

**29th AUSTRALIAN GRAND PRIX AT SANDOWN PARK**

63 laps of 1.92 miles — 121 miles

| | |
|---|---|
| 1. Jack Brabham (Brabham) | 1 hr 15′ 19.2″ |
| 2. Bib Stillwell (Brabham) | 1 hr 15′ 31.1″ |
| 3. John Youl (Cooper) | 1 hr 15′ 34.1″ |
| 4. Tim Mayer (Cooper) | 1 hr 16′ 6.5″ |
| 5. Denis Hulme (Brabham) | 60 laps |
| 6. Jim Palmer (Cooper) | 60 laps |

**Fastest lap:** J. Brabham 1′ 9.5″, 99.83 mph

## Warwick Farm

This was the scene of Brabham's first victory a year ago, and it is a measure of his improvement that his best practice time this year was three seconds faster than his lap record shared with Surtees' Lola; indeed the race average for the first four cars was higher than the old record. It was Matich, though, who took the honours in practice, gaining pole position in his Brabham with a rousing 1′ 37″, beating both Hulme and Brabham by 0.2″ and reserving the front row for the marque.

After tailoring the car to his liking Graham Hill took his borrowed Brabham round in 1′ 37.7″, sharing a place in the second row with Bruce McLaren. Back to the last row but one, drivers had beaten the lap record, and this included Leo Geoghegan's Lotus 27, the 1,500 cc Ford engine sufficing to get him round in 1′ 38.9″, and another notable was Frank Gardner's Brabham Junior which got round in 1′ 39.7″.

Hulme felt more than a little vulnerable when his engine stalled as the flag dropped, but everyone avoided him and it was Brabham who led on the first lap with Matich challenging, followed by Hill, McLaren and Mayer. The American damaged the nose of his car on McLaren's back wheel, and dropped back very slightly, but the real fun was going on in the lead, when Matich nipped past Jack braking into the hairpin. Success must have gone to his head, for two laps later Frank spun his car coming out of the hairpin and broke the suspension, and although he limped round for a few more laps his lead had gone and once more Jack was in front.

McLaren and Hill were tussling wheel to wheel for second place a second behind Brabham, with Mayer some

*Jack Brabham was victorious on home ground, winning three Australian races; his marque won all four, but McLaren won the series through superiority in New Zealand*

*At Lakeside, Youl drifts his "pencil line" Cooper through Shell ahead of McLaren and Hulme*

*Denny Hulme was unrewarded in Australia, settling for two fifth places only and retiring at Lakeside. He sold his Brabham to Lex Davison who will be using it in the 1965 series*

Frank Matich drove his Total-sponsored Brabham really fast to worry the European experts at times, but press-on tactics caused three retirements. He nursed his car to finish third at Longford

four seconds behind, and behind them Hulme was making mighty efforts to catch the leaders after his disastrous start, but the pace was too hot for him to get within 20 seconds of the flying four so he contented himself staying in front of Stillwell and waiting for the leaders to retire!

Midway through the race Hill, bothered by brake grabbing, made an excursion on to the grass letting Mayer through, and after that he settled back to watch the race from a more comfortable viewpoint, secure in the knowledge that he was a mile in front of Hulme. Up front, McLaren hustled and harried, but Brabham made no mistakes and crossed the line less than half a second in front.

**RESULTS**

**WARWICK FARM INTERNATIONAL 100**

45 laps of 2.25 miles — 101.25 miles

| | |
|---|---|
| 1. Jack Brabham (Brabham) | 1 hr 13′ 45.1″ |
| 2. Bruce McLaren (Cooper) | 1 hr 13′ 45.5″ |
| 3. Tim Mayer (Cooper) | 1 hr 13′ 56.9″ |
| 4. Graham Hill (Brabham) | 1 hr 14′ 09.1″ |
| 5. Denis Hulme (Brabham) | 1 hr 14′ 41.6″ |
| 6. Bib Stillwell (Brabham) | 1 hr 15′ 05.3″ |

**Fastest lap:** Bruce McLaren, 1′ 37.4″ 83.10 mph

Tim Mayer, in his last race, comes up pass team-mate Bruce McLaren

# Lakeside International

The second last round of the Tasman Cup Series was run at Lakeside on February 23rd, and drew a small but select band of drivers and cars. Both Brabham and McLaren entered and brought with them similar cars for their "second string" drivers, Denis Hulme and Tim Mayer.

The Lakeside Circuit, some 24 miles from Brisbane, is 1.5 miles to the lap and features two very tight loops in addition to fast left and right handers. The lap record stood at 59.6″ (John Youl). Practice on Saturday was conducted in alternating patches of sunshine and showers, which made things rather trying for everyone.

John Youl in the "old" pencil line Cooper with twin plug head set the ball rolling with a 59.6″. Fellow Australian, Frank Matich, in a Repco-Brabham did 59.1″ then 58.9″. The American, Tim Mayer, learnt the circuit rapidly and turned in a 59.0″. Brabham and McLaren were doing consistent 1 minute laps.

A heavy shower spoiled the chances of faster laps until later in the afternoon. First out onto the circuit was Matich and with a dry surface and no traffic he turned in a 58.7″. Mayer now got down to 58.8″, which at the time was wrongly announced as 58.7″. This was corrected however and neither Matich nor Mayer were to better these times. However neither Brabham nor McLaren could equal these and so at the conclusion of practice Matich held pole position with 58.7″, Mayer next with 58.8″ and Brabham third fastest on 58.9″.

Race day dawned fine, but also very humid as the sun had its effect on the waterlogged circuit. The grid for the International was set out for cars in pairs, and we therefore saw Matich and Mayer on the front row, with Brabham and Youl on the second, and McLaren and Hulme comprising the third.

As the flag dropped, Matich made a terrific start, consolidating the advantage obtained from the fastest practice lap. He recorded a standing of 1′ 5.5″, a full half second faster than the next man, Mayer. Matich kept up this pace for the next six laps with Mayer sitting in his exhaust pipe, recording extremely consistent times. On lap 7, however, the Australian's race was run, when a con rod left home rather abruptly; the disconsolate Matich parked the car opposite the pits and watched Mayer shoot into the lead.

Brabham had sorted himself by this time and was now threatening Mayer who still held tenaciously to first spot. The American was showing that he was a very real threat indeed as he turned in 11 laps under the 1 minute mark with only 0.5″ variation throughout. Regrettably for Mayer, this fine performance was to go unrewarded, as on lap 13 the oil pressure zeroed leaving him no alternative but to pull out.

With Mayer off the scene Brabham forged into an unapproachable lead; behind him Youl, McLaren and Hulme squabbled for second spot. McLaren, handicapped by an injured left hand, was apparently playing it safe, but he still found that Youl and Hulme kept him busy.

Youl made things a little easier for the pair of New Zealanders by dropping back with a "fluffy" motor as Hulme got past McLaren. Frank Gardner led the under 1500 class with the Brabham-Ford, whilst Glynn Scott in a Lotus 27 held off Glass' Lotus 27 with twin-cam Ford motor.

The race had now become a procession with Brabham effortlessly in the lead. McLaren had repassed Hulme and Youl tagged along in 4th position.

On lap 57 however, Hulme shunted McLaren at the Karrussel and the latter shot off into the scenery. Fortunately the scenery was not damaging and McLaren got back onto the circuit to find that both Hulme and Youl had passed. Hulme had deranged the nose of the Brabham in this "boo-boo", consequently retiring. This moved Youl into 2nd place, McLaren into 3rd and Gardner into 4th slot.

So after 66 laps the wily Brabham took out the chequered flag having averaged 89 mph for 99 miles and put in a new lap record of 58.7″ which of course equalled Matich's practice time. Brabham gathered in another 9 points for the Tasman Cup, bringing his tally to 33, but McLaren collected 4 for 3rd making his 37.

**RESULTS**

1. Jack Brabham (Repco-Brabham 2.5)
2. John Youl (Cooper-Climax 2.5)
3. Bruce McLaren (Cooper-Climax 2.5)
4. Frank Gardner (Brabham 1500)
5. Tony Shelley (Lola-Climax 2.5)

**Race time:** 66′ 46.4″—89 mph
**Fastest lap:** Jack Brabham, 58.7″, 91.8 mph.

# South Pacific GP

With three wins in a row, Brabham could not improve upon his score of points in Australia (best three out of four to count in New Zealand and in Australia) so McLaren had already clinched the Tasman Championship when the crews got to Longford, in Tasmania. Even so a needle-match was expected on this fast circuit, but the entire meeting was cast into gloom when Timmy Mayer crashed during the first practice session, and was killed. Apparently his car became airborne at one point and landed badly, sliding into a tree.

Longford is a road-racing circuit and the fastest in Australia, cars reaching 175 mph on the back straight and lapping at close on 115 mph. The 4½-mile track has two fast straights and a couple of slow corners, but bumps in the road were troubling all the drivers. McLaren did not continue to practice after Mayer's crash, and started from the back row of the grid. This left the Brabhams in complete command, with Jack in pole position at 2′ 24.2″, followed by Graham Hill at 2′ 24.3″ in the "old" Brabham, beating Matich's new model by half a second. Matich, incidentally, had borrowed an engine from Brabham having ruined his own at Lakeside. Lex Davison bought Hulme's Brabham, leaving Hulme a non-starter, but used his Cooper for this race and returned 2′ 26″ to share the second row with Bib Stillwell's Brabham.

True to form, Brabham led on the first lap with Hill in close attendance, followed by Stillwell and Matich; McLaren was rocketing through from the back of the grid to seventh place behind Davison and Youl, and the next time round he was fifth after Brabham, Hill, Matich and Stillwell. Matich was already challenging Hill but gave up the attempt after four laps, probably being more interested in finishing, and soon McLaren was pressing him after disposing of Stillwell. Youl left the course rather rapidly to rejoin the race two places down, but he soon passed Palmer and Shelley to make up this leeway.

Still McLaren was trying hard, and he passed Matich when the Brabham's engine began to sound a bit rough, so the order on lap ten was Brabham, followed by Hill at 5 seconds, followed by McLaren at 10 seconds, then Matich, Stillwell, Youl, Palmer and Shelley. At 13 laps, just over half distance, Brabham's lead had been narrowed, and Hill was obviously working very hard with his bigger car to make any impression. McLaren wasn't getting any closer however, and Matich was wondering how comfortable was his advantage over Stillwell as his engine misfired at high revs.

High drama set in at 20 laps when Brabham pulled off with transmission trouble, so it was a delighted Hill who came through in front on the 21st lap, with four laps remaining to the flag. McLaren was still trying desperately hard and he cut the lead down to 10 seconds at the end, while behind him Matich was nursing a sick engine and trying to stave Stillwell off at the same time. Well, he got to the line alright, a tenth of a second in front of Stillwell, and Youl passed Davison's Cooper into fifth place just before the end. Frank Gardner had driven a tidy race in his Brabham Junior to finish a lap and a half down, in ninth place.

**RESULTS**
**SOUTH PACIFIC GRAND PRIX AT LONGFORD**
25 laps of 4.5 miles — 112½ miles

| | |
|---|---|
| 1. Graham Hill (Brabham) | 1 hr 0′ 25.8″ |
| 2. Bruce McLaren (Cooper) | 1 hr 0′ 35.1″ |
| 3. Frank Matich (Brabham) | 1 hr 1′ 3.3″ |
| 4. Bib Stillwell (Cooper) | 1 hr 1′ 3.4″ |
| 5. John Youl (Cooper) | 1 hr 1′ 26″ |
| 6. Lex Davison (Cooper) | 1 hr 1′ 30.7″ |

**Fastest lap:** Bruce McLaren. 2′ 23.3″, 113.05 mph

# Tripmaster to be Exact

The exact distance between two points is a variable which troubles rally drivers, firms' accountants, and fuel economy experts alike, for rarely do two trip-meters tally over a distance of 10 miles or more. The problem has been solved now by Halda Limited, makers of the Speedpilot, who have introduced a new Tripmaster claimed to be accurate to 0.2 per cent, or less than 400 yards in 100 miles.

The meter has been designed after co-operation with the Volvo and Saab competition departments, and its most obvious use is in rally cars, although it has application in any case where payment is made on a mileage basis. A refinement of the Tripmaster is three settings which enable it to record distance covered, to run in 'neutral' without recording, or else to subtract from the total when the car is re-tracing part of the route after a navigational error, so obliterating the incorrect reading.

Distance recorders fitted as original equipment are rarely accurate within one per cent, and are often as much as five miles out in every hundred; this discrepancy increases with tyrewear,and the equipment becomes totally unreliable if different tyres are fitted (low profile type for instance). The Tripmeter, therefore, incorporates variators which can be fitted (after experiment) to suit different tyre sizes exactly, which is ideal in rally conditions where several different types of tyre may be used on a short period of time.

The Halda is illuminated, and costs £17 10s.

**They've made a Tasman Formula 2.5 litre. What next?**

# A REPCO FORMULA 1 ENGINE?

Engineer Frank Hallam

Designer Phil Irving

REPCO announced in mid-September the most important development yet in its Repco-Brabham racing program — complete V8 racing engines designed and produced in its own factories. The first engine produced is a Tasman Formula 2.5 litre. Will a 3-litre come next, for the 1966 Formula 1?

The 2.5 is designed for about 250 bhp at 8000 rpm, with useful power through the wide limits of 5000 and 8500 rpm. The company observes that substantial power at lower speeds will be of special value on the short circuits usual in Australian racing.

The new machinery is officially designated the Repco-Brabham Type 620. It is for installation in chassis designed to carry Repco-Brabhams based on the Coventry-Climax four-cylinder.

The Repco-Brabham Type 620 . . . 250 bhp at 8000 rpm. It won't be used in the coming season unless someone forces the issue.

The Type 620 has undergone comprehensive testing and development at the Repco engine laboratory in Richmond, Victoria, but will not be raced in the coming season in the Tasman Formula events unless competitors come up with engines of a new type and force the issue.

The first appearance is more likely to be in sports car racing, in 4.3-litre form, since it is readily adaptable to production in any capacity up to this size. By the following season the 2.5-litre version will be available to anyone requiring one, an arrangement regarded as fairest and in the best interests of the sport.

The 4.3 version is of interest to sports car racing competitors overseas as well as in Australia. Will the day come when Australian-built Formula 1 engines find themselves in crates labelled "Export"?

The decision to build the V8 engines was taken in February 1964, when it seemed obvious that the reserve of four-cylinder Climaxes would be certain to dry up well within the lifetime of the Tasman 2.5-litre formula. It was also recognised that the designing and building of racing engines, from the ground up, was the logical next stage in the Repco-Brabham racing program.

Only 51 weeks later, on March 21, 1965, the first engine roared on a dynamometer. The V8 configuration was chosen, because it was felt that the limits for the development of a four-cylinder engine had been very nearly reached in the Coventry-Climax-based 2.5 litre, and the only avenue for progress was multiplication of cylinders to provide greater piston area.

Following the success of the Repco-Brabhams, both in competition and as a research project for the technical improvement of their bread-and-butter lines, the Repco directors decided to take the important step of designing and building a complete engine.

The design assignment was placed in the hands of Phil Irving, who is internationally known as an engine designer, with the project as a whole under Frank Hallam, MSAE, chief engineer of the Repco Engine Parts group of companies. He has been prominent on the technical development side of motor sport in Australia for many years.

It was decided to short-circuit one costly foundry opera-

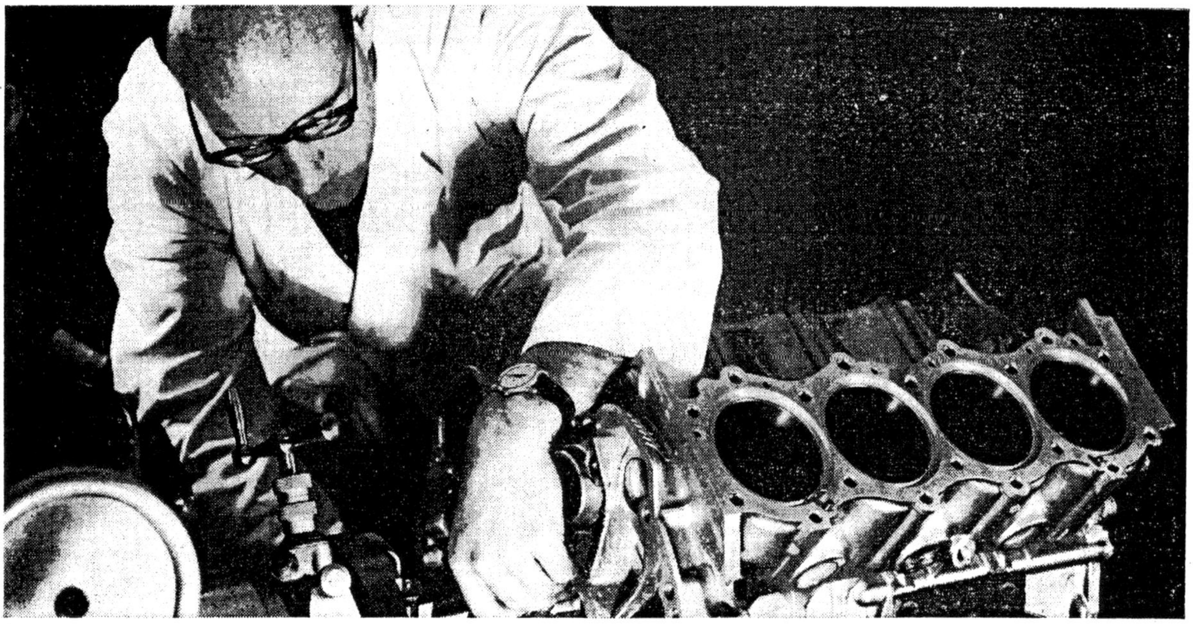

Peter Holinger, a Repco engineer, reboring the rear main bearing housing of the new engine to take the oil seal housing. The Type 620 was designed for fuel injection but was first tested with carburettors. At latest report fuel injection gear was under test.

tion by using an existing light-alloy crankcase, but even this component had to be greatly modified. With this as a basis, the design was worked out by Phil Irving for the cylinder head, timing cases, sump, oil pumps and other items calling for complex pattern-making and specialised magnesium-alloy techniques.

He also designed the crankshaft, which was machined by Laystall Engineering, a leading British specialist in this work, from a billet of EN52 nitriding steel.

The crankcase and cylinder block casting provides for wide latitude in engine capacity, from the present 2.5 litres up to 4.3 litres, which should make it adaptable for a really formidable sports-racing car.

The Type 620 has single camshaft and vertical valves for each bank. Compression ratio is 11:1. The camshafts have five bearings, carried in light-alloy blocks. Valve gear has been run up to 10,000 rpm on a test rig and performed satisfactorily.

The engine has been designed for fuel injection, the system under consideration being a new one which is very light and simple. Meanwhile, testing went on with Weber carburettors pending arrival of the injection equipment. At latest report, the injection system is now under test.

**BRIEF SPECIFICATIONS:**

Construction: Light alloy castings throughout, configuration being a 90 deg. V8 with one overhead camshaft per bank, chain-driven Overall dimensions are to suit Repco-Brabham or other cars designed for the Coventry-Climax-based four-cylinder engine now no longer in production.

Capacity, 2498 cc. Bore and stroke, 85 mm x 55 mm. Compression ratio, 11:1.

Fuel injection.

Designed maximum engine speed, 8500 rpm or possibly higher, developing approximately 250 bhp at 8000 rpm. Useful power range will be between the wide limits of 5500 and 8500 rpm.

Length overall (excluding flywheel), 25½in.
Width over cylinder heads, 21in.
Width at bell-housing, 17¼in.
Height overall (not including carburettors), 23in.
Depth below crankshaft axis, 6¼in.
Cylinder heads to crankshaft axis, 15½in.

# WORLD CHAMPIONS SECOND YEAR IN SUCCESSION!

## REPCO-BRABHAM SUCCESSES 1966 AND 1967

### Constructor's Championship

| 1966 | 1967 |
|---|---|
| Repco-Brabham | Repco-Brabham |

### World Championship of Drivers

| 1966 | 1967 |
|---|---|
| 1st Jack Brabham | 1st Denny Hulme |
| 4th Denny Hulme | 2nd Jack Brabham |

### Formula 1 Grand Prix Series

**1966**

|  |  |
|---|---|
| Belgian Grand Prix | — 4th |
| French Grand Prix | — 1st & 3rd |
| British Grand Prix | — 1st & 2nd |
| Dutch Grand Prix | — 1st |
| German Grand Prix | — 1st |
| Italian Grand Prix | — 3rd |
| Mexican Grand Prix | — 2nd & 3rd |

**1967**

|  |  |
|---|---|
| South African Grand Prix | — 4th & 6th |
| Monaco Grand Prix | — 1st |
| Dutch Grand Prix | — 2nd & 3rd |
| French Grand Prix | — 1st & 2nd |
| British Grand Prix | — 2nd & 4th |
| German Grand Prix | — 1st & 2nd |
| Canadian Grand Prix | — 1st & 2nd |
| Italian Grand Prix | — 2nd |
| American Grand Prix | — 3rd & 5th |
| Mexican Grand Prix | — 2nd & 3rd |

The Repco designed and built racing engine that powered these cars is one example of Repco automotive engineering skills. That Repco can design, develop and manufacture such an engine in Australia is not only a credit to its own skills and resources, but to Australian technology generally.

**REPCO** where the standard is perfection

Manufacturers, merchandisers, exporters of automotive components, accessories, hand and machine tools, service equipment for transport, industry and agriculture.

# Repco-BRABHAM WINS AGAIN

## IN EUROPE

REPCO-BRABHAM FORMULA JUNIOR CARS HAVE WON: BRANDS HATCH, AINTREE, SILVERSTONE, CRYSTAL PALACE, RHEIMS.

## IN AUSTRALIA

REPCO-BRABHAM INTERCONTINENTAL CARS HAVE WON: AUSTRALIAN GRAND PRIX, N.S.W. ROAD RACING CHAMPIONSHIP, LOWOOD, SANDOWN.

The Repco-Brabham is a further step that keeps Repco abreast, and often ahead, of international automotive developments.

**WHERE THE STANDARD IS PERFECTION**

Automotive parts for all makes and models

4777

# British Benefit

## 1959 R.A.C. British Grand Prix

*Jack Brabham showed world champion class in recording his second **grande epreuve** win of the season*

***STARTING GRID:***

J. Brabham (Cooper-Climax) 1′ 58·0″ — R. Salvadori (Aston Martin) 1′ 58·0″ — H. Shell (B.R.M.) 1′ 59·2″

M. Trintignant (Cooper-Climax) 1′ 59·2″ — M. Gregory (Cooper-Climax) 1′ 59·4″

C. Shelby (Aston Martin) 1′ 59·6″ — S. Moss (B.R.M.) 1′ 59·6″ — B. McLaren (Cooper-Climax) 1′ 59·6″

G. Hill (Lotus-Climax) 2′ 00·0″ — J. Bonnier (B.R.M.) 2′ 00·0″

R. Flockhart (B.R.M.) 2′ 00·2″ — I. Ireland (Lotus-Climax) 2′ 02·8″ — I. Burgess (Cooper-Maserati) 2′ 03·0″

B. Naylor (J.B.W.-Maserati) 2′ 03·0″ — J. E. G. Fairman (Cooper-Climax) 2′ 04·2″

C. Bristow (Cooper-Borgward) 2′ 04·4″ — C. A. S. Brooks (Vanwall) 2′ 04·6″ — I. Bueb (Cooper-Borgward) 2′ 04·8″

H. Herrmann (Cooper-Maserati) 2′ 05·6″ — F. d'Orey (Maserati) 2′ 05·6″

H. C. Taylor (Cooper-Climax) 2′ 05·6″ — D. R. Piper (Lotus-Climax) 2′ 06·0″ — P. Ashdown (Cooper-Climax) 2′ 05·2″

M. J. C. Taylor (Cooper-Climax) 2′ 07·0″

A FEW years ago it would have been unthinkable that a Grand Prix counting for the international Championship could not only be run with a virtually complete field of British cars, but could also have been absorbingly interesting. The withdrawal of the Ferrari team due to what was hazily described as a metal workers' strike left the serious contenders in the British Grand Prix as Cooper-Climax, B.R.M., Aston Martin and Lotus. There was a lone Vanwall making its first outing of the 1959 season in the hands of Brooks, and two red-painted Cooper-Maseratis of the Scuderia Centro-Sud, with a supporting cast consisting of Fritz D'Orey's Maserati and an assorted selection of Formula 2 machinery.

A full works team of Coopers was competing, headed by Jack Brabham, with McLaren and Gregory in supporting roles. Stirling Moss was at the wheel of the British Racing Partnership's B.R.M., and in addition there were three works cars in the hands of Harry Shell, Joachim Bonnier and Ron Flockhart. Roy Salvadori and Carroll Shelby had the wheels of the Aston Martins, while Graham Hill and Innes Ireland were in the Formula 1 Lotuses. The Centro-Sud Cooper-Maseratis were driven by Burgess and Herrmann, and Brian Naylor had his J.B.W.-Maserati.

### Practising

Thursday's practice session was undertaken in rainy weather and the stability of the B.R.M. was proved by Stirling Moss's fast practice time under the circumstances of 2′ 8″. Despite a rainy morning on Friday the course had dried out for Grand Prix practising in the afternoon, and a clearer picture of the performance of the cars on this tight circuit was given. Jack Brabham immediately began to circulate with a deal of determination. After breaking 2′ he progressively reduced his time to 1′ 58″ and then called it a day. The other drivers were slower at getting into their stride, with the B.R.M.s, the Aston Martins and the lone Vanwall all having rectative periods at the pits after short trials. Eventually, however, both the B.R.M.s and the Aston Martins, particularly Salvadori in the latter case, started to break 2′. To everyone's surprise it was Salvadori who became the sensation of the session by equalling Brabham's time of 1′ 58″. Stirling Moss, who was apparently not completely satisfied with his car, could do no better than 1′ 59·6″ which put him in the third row of the grid. The Vanwall continued to have misfiring and braking troubles to the end of the session, and Brooks could do no better than 2′ 4·6″, rather slower than the Formula 2 Cooper-Borgward of Chris Bristow.

### Saturday

The early hours of Saturday morning were all too Liverpudlian in aspect. The rain which had departed the previous afternoon had returned with a vengeance, and caused no surprise to the locals who had not apparently heard that the rest of England was suffering from a prolonged drought. However, well before midday and the curtain-raising sports car race the rain had stopped and the track had dried out. As in the Grand Prix, Jack Brabham was the favourite for the sports car race having returned a time of 2′ 3·6″ in his Cooper-Climax. Graham Hill and Stirling Moss appeared evenly matched on the other front places of the grid with 2′ 4·4″ and 2′ 4·6″ best practice time. Many of Moss's followers were confident that he could pull out that little bit of extra on the day which would allow him to pip both his rivals. It was not to be. As the flag fell Moss stalled his engine and Clark, in the Border Reivers Lister-Jaguar, had to dodge smartly between him and the pit counter in order to avoid being baulked, while Greenall shot through from the fourth row, failed to notice that Moss had not started, and shunted him very solidly up the course. The push was apparently what Moss needed, for the car fired and he was away towards the tail of the field! Poor Greenall, on the contrary, had made a mess of his Lotus and had practically dislocated his neck into the bargain.

Brabham and Hill had been well away, and at the end of the first lap it was the Lotus in the lead by a comfortable margin from the Cooper. Hill continued to pull away for three laps, settling down with a five-second lead thereafter. At the end of the first lap Moss came to his pit, had the bodywork pulled off his rear wheels, a quick inspection, and was away 1′ 10″ behind the leaders. At five laps the order was still Hill, Brabham, Stacey (Lotus), Blond (Lister), Halford (Lister), Flockhart (Tojeiro), Uren (Lister), Clark (Lister). On lap six Brabham began to make an effort to overhaul the Lotus and he steadily closed up until he was right on Hill's tail, a position he maintained until the twelfth lap when, driving with gay abandon, he took the lead and a few yards of grass at Tatts only to be overtaken again on the subsequent lap as rain started to fall on some parts of the circuit.

Behind, Ivor Bueb had come strongly through the field: after being seventh on lap two he was pressing Stacey's Lotus by lap eight. Moss also was doing a field-cleaving act; lapping in 2′ 4″ or thereabouts, he was lying eleventh on lap six, ninth on lap ten, and shaping to move into eighth place on lap twelve when his car caught fire at Anchor Crossing having apparently fractured an oil pipe in the earlier impact, and Stirling was lucky to clamber out of the car uninjured. The rain which started to fall on lap thirteen did not spread to the whole of the circuit for some time. On lap fifteen an extraordinary fracas occurred at Melling Crossing when Peter Blond, driving the Ecurie Ecosse Lister, lost control and somersaulted, disturbing Ron Flockhart, who was immediately behind in the same stable's Tojeiro, to such an extent that he charged the straw bales. This all occurred as the leaders were arriving to lap the cars in question and although Hill, who had had the prescience to fit rain tyres, was able to negotiate the melee, Brabham went off course as did a number of others; indeed one report indicated that no less than nine cars were on the grass at one stage. By the time Brabham had got moving again Stacey was close to him and passed him on the penultimate lap, so that Lotuses scored a one-two victory.

### The Grand Prix

During the lengthy lunch interval the weather improved considerably and the circuit was dry once more for the start of the 12th British Grand Prix. *Despite* the preponderance of green in different shades the starting grid was a brave sight. The fall of the flag saw Brabham leap straight into the lead with the two B.R.M.s of Shell and Bonnier close behind. At the end of the first lap the order was Brabham, Shell, Bonnier, Gregory, Trintignant, Moss, McLaren, Hill and Salvadori. Drama was not long in coming, for on the second lap Carroll Shelby came into his pit to enquire modestly if everything was all right since he had been deluged with oil from an over-filled oil tank. He was quickly despatched back into the race, but his team mate Salvadori was suffering from the same trouble and came in on lap three to change his goggles for a visor. For the rest of the race it appeared that splashes of oil were blowing on to him, for he could be seen wiping the visor on several occasions. Brabham in the meantime had moved quickly into his stride, lapping at just over two minutes, and pulling swiftly away from Shell in the pursuing B.R.M. Stirling Moss was making up for a slow start, picking off Trintignant on the second lap and McLaren on the third. Gregory, lying in fourth place showed no great willingness to be picked and kept ahead of Moss so that the two of them passed Bonnier's B.R.M. on lap six, before Moss eventually passed the American on lap seven to take third position. He then closed rapidly on Harry Shell, and on lap nine went into second place 40″ behind Brabham who was still driving unhurriedly at around the two minute mark.

During the course of Stirling's progression up the field a war of attrition was waged between Bonnier, Trintignant, McLaren and Hill, with Flockhart driving most pleasantly not far behind. Salvadori's early pit stop had dropped him from tenth position to fifteenth, and he also was gradually working back up the field although with the impediment of the spraying oil he was achieving nothing like the lap times which he had in practice. With ten laps gone, therefore, the order was Brabham, 14″ ahead of Moss, then Shell, Trintignant, who had put on a burst of speed to overtake Bonnier and Gregory, Bonnier, McLaren. Gregory, Hill, Flockhart, Salvadori. In his hurry Salvadori had dented the air intake of his car, although not sufficiently to cause overheating.

On the eleventh lap Hill spun his Lotus at Tatts Corner and let himself get into the sights of Salvadori, who had just passed Flockhart. In watching the progression of the Aston Martin it was truly remarkable to see its tremendous braking power and stable cornering. Indeed, had its acceleration matched its deceleration there would have been no holding the new Feltham bolide. On lap 14, for instance, Salvadori lapped a slower car and passed Hill's Lotus from being some 20 yards behind both on the approach to Tatts Corner. As they accelerated away Hill was able to re-pass the Aston Martin quite comfortably. On the 13th lap Brooks brought in the Vanwall which, apart from misfiring, had a recurrence of its braking troubles, and after a brief inspection the car was pushed away. Not an auspicious outing for Mr. Vandervell but, we are sure, not sufficient to discourage him.

### The pace quickens

At the front of the field the pace was hotting up slightly, with Brabham taking his times down to just under two minutes and pulling out to some 17″ lead on Moss by lap 20. A battle royal now developed for third, fourth and fifth places with Trintignant, Shell and McLaren driving nose to tail for seven or eight laps and interchanging frequently, with the final sort-out becoming McLaren. Trintignant, Shell. Only ten cars now remained on the same lap, and the Formula 2 race was being led by Chris Bristow in the B.R.P. Cooper-Borgward ahead of Ivor Bueb in the stable car.

The presence of Stirling Moss behind him was having its effect on Brabham, who steadily built up speed and increased the race average. Although always controlled, the Cooper was noticeably light at the rear on the sharper corners. Conversely the B.R.M.s were extremely stable and gradually getting quicker on their cornering as the fuel levels went down. Trintignant and Shell travelled in close company for many laps until Shell slightly overdid things at Tatts on the 32nd lap and dropped back. Behind him another private war was taking place between Bonnier, Gregory and Salvadori. These three passed and re-passed until on lap 37, exactly half-way through the race, Bonnier failed to appear and later toured into the pits with a dead engine. And so at 40 laps, just over half distance, the order was Brabham (Cooper-Climax) 1: 19′ 59·8″, Moss (B.R.M.) 1: 20′ 11·8″, McLaren (Cooper) 1: 20′ 45·8″, Shell (B.R.M.) 1: 21′ 1·6″, Trintignant (Cooper), Gregory (Cooper), Salvadori (Aston Martin), and a lap in arrears Flockhart, Shelby and Hill. Between laps 35 and 45 Brabham's lead over Moss had remained more or less constant at 12″, but from lap 45 onwards Moss started to make his big effort. It later transpired that from about lap 35 Brabham had been aware of tread-wear on his tyres and had no inclination to go any faster. It is possible, therefore, that if Moss had made his attempt ten laps earlier the result might well have been different. As it was he progressively trimmed half-seconds off the Australian's lead until on lap 48 it was only 8″. Then out went the sign (that many had expected even before this) to indicate to Moss that he must come in for tyres. The car was at rest in the pits for 34″ while both rear tyres were changed, but the slowing down involved put the B.R.M. back to 51″ in arrears of the Cooper, and only 13″ ahead of McLaren's speeding sister car. Moss immediately forged back into the fray and began to make up ground, although not apparently at a rate that would yield a serious prospect of victory.

By lap 53 all but the first four cars had been lapped, and Brabham had slowed down to a lap time of approximately two minutes. On lap 58 Gregory brought the third works Cooper into the pits and Hill's Lotus was visibly slowing. By lap 60 the cars lying in fifth, sixth and seventh positions, namely Trintignant, Salvadori and Shelby, were a lap ahead of their rivals while being a lap in arrears of the leaders. Moss was now gaining on Brabham one or two seconds every lap, and had opened out the gap on McLaren to 33″ by lap 64. McLaren in turn was 22″ ahead of Shell. The question now was whether any of the Coopers would be forced to stop for a tyre change, which would, due to the bolt-on wheels, have put paid to their chances. Despite the fact that at one stage a signal appeared purporting to call Brabham in for tyres the Australian did not come, and it can only be assumed that it was a safety-first deception on the part of the Cooper pit staff to try and slow Moss down.

### Moss in again

With ten laps left to run Moss was still 35″ behind Brabham and gaining at a maximum of 2″ a lap, so all hope seemed to be lost. This was further confirmed when on lap 67 he came into the pits for a top-up of fuel. At the time it seemed extraordinary that if there were any doubt about his fuel capacity the pit staff had not topped up the tank at the time of his tyre change. It later transpired that he finished the race with plenty of fuel in hand and the misfiring which he experienced, and which indicated a low fuel level, was caused by fuel from the rear tank not passing through to the side tanks quickly enough after he had changed over. The mystery nearly cost him dearly, for as he left the pits after a quick stop McLaren went past to take second position. For one lap only he was there, and then on lap 69 Moss re-passed, but the young New Zealander showed no inclination to be thrown off and followed Moss closely to the end of the race. On lap 70 Aston Martins had a blow when Shelby was forced to retire with ignition trouble while placing seventh, but all attention was focused on the duel for second place. That Stirling was really being harried quickly became evident. Not only did he put in two laps at 1′ 57·6″ and then 1′ 57″ dead, looking more untidy than at any time during the race; but despite this scintillating speed, the New Zealander was still there; and indeed on the ultimate lap he also circulated in 1′ 57″ to get right back on Moss's tail and cross the line only one-fifth of a second behind the B.R.M. He also took half a championship point for sharing the fastest lap. Only these three cars remained on the same lap, since a pit stop for tyres by Harry Shell on lap 66 had cost him 30″ and put him back onto the same lap as Trintignant and Salvadori. It was nevertheless a good day for B.R.M. as well as for Cooper, the Bourne concern taking second and fourth place while the Surbiton/Dorking outfit took, first, third and fifth. After its very fast practice lap times the Aston Martin did not fulfil expectations, but the trouble was not serious, and given a little bit more power to offset the very light weight of the Coopers the tremendous stopping and cornering power of the Astons will begin to show dividends.

# BRABHAM
## a special section on *The Machines and the Men Behind Them*

*1966: A former World Champion returns to the top, dominating two formulas with equal parts of straight thinking and hard driving.*

*CENTER SPREAD: Winner and again champion, Jack Brabham and his Brabham-Repco Formula 1 car at Zandvoort. Color photo by Dennis Cipnic. RIGHT: The top Grand Prix car of 1966 illustrated in detail by artist Werner Bührer.*

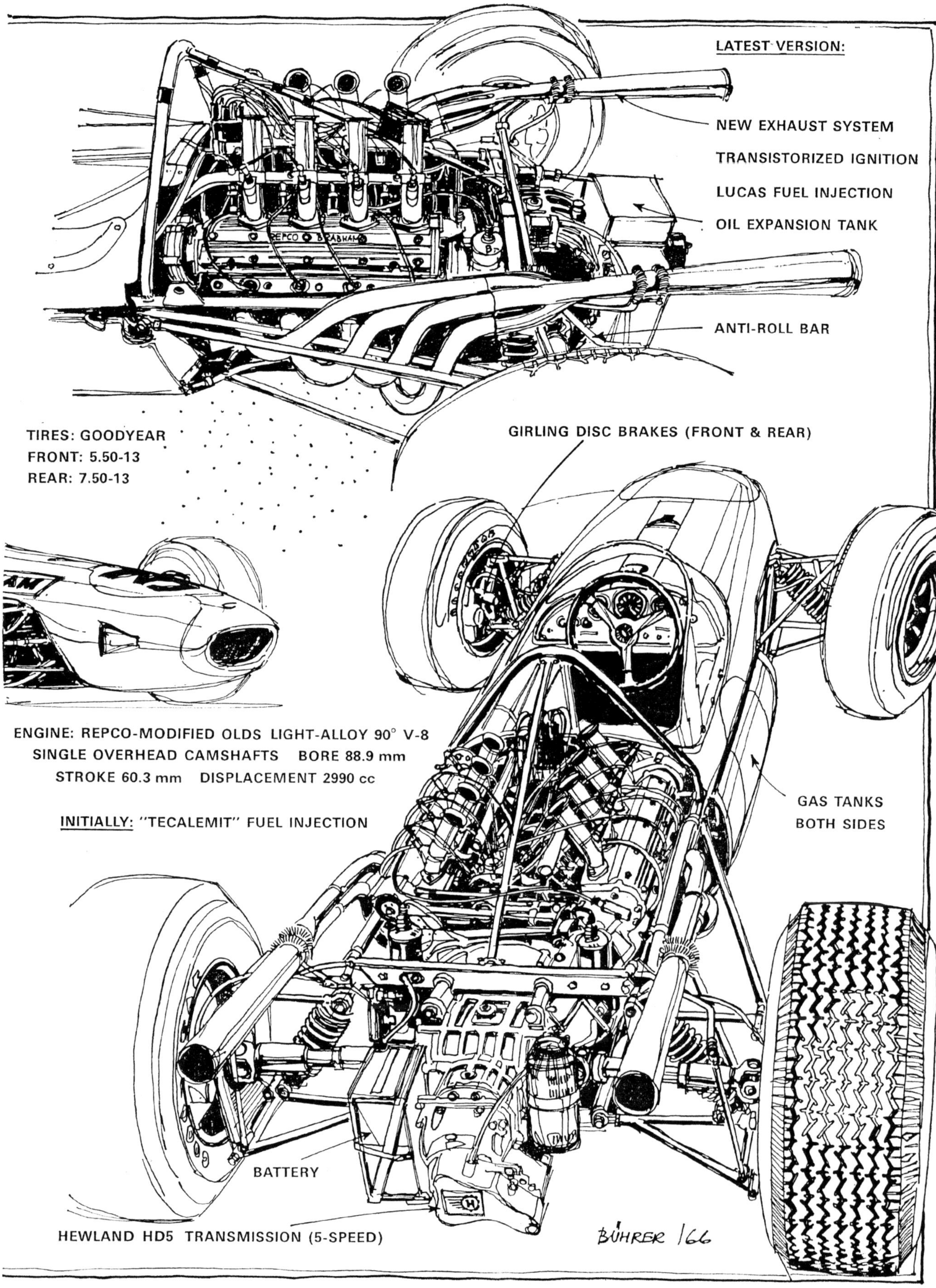
LATEST VERSION:
NEW EXHAUST SYSTEM
TRANSISTORIZED IGNITION
LUCAS FUEL INJECTION
OIL EXPANSION TANK
ANTI-ROLL BAR
TIRES: GOODYEAR
FRONT: 5.50-13
REAR: 7.50-13
GIRLING DISC BRAKES (FRONT & REAR)
ENGINE: REPCO-MODIFIED OLDS LIGHT-ALLOY 90° V-8
SINGLE OVERHEAD CAMSHAFTS BORE 88.9 mm
STROKE 60.3 mm DISPLACEMENT 2990 cc
INITIALLY: "TECALEMIT" FUEL INJECTION
GAS TANKS
BOTH SIDES
BATTERY
HEWLAND HD5 TRANSMISSION (5-SPEED)
BÜHRER 166

Most of the time you will find Brabham senior at Coopers helping to prepare the Formula One cars. Jack loves every moment of it for he is a first rate engineer as well as an extremely good test driver.

Aston Martin had their eye on him to test and drive their new Formula One cars, but he preferred to remain with the Cooper team, the firm that gave him his first opportunity in this country.

A new Brabham interest is a small garage, not far from the Kingston by-pass, which will most likely become a tuning establishment.

Brabham came into motor racing quite by chance, in fact he was really *talked* into it by Johnny Schonberg, one-time American speedway ace, but it was the engineering side of racing that appealed most of all, at first. The two were on their way to Darwin from Sidney during the summer of 1946 and to pass the time away Schonberg related tales of his midget car racing days, Jack, who knew nothing at all about car racing, was only mildly interested.

Stopping at Brisbane, Schonberg spotted an advertisement for midget car racing, one of the first in Australia, and dragged Brabham along to see it, much against his will. This was his first experience of any type of racing and as he expressed it, "I was frightened to death"; for the remainder of the trip, which lasted two months, Johnny Schonberg was continually talking about racing. Finally on arrival back in Sydney they decided to form a racing partnership and build a midget car at Jack's modest workshop, which Schonberg was to drive.

Things didn't quite work out as planned. In the end it was Brabham who raced the car and within twelve months had made a name for himself by winning the New South Wales Championship. He continued in speedway racing until 1951 taking the South Australian and Australian Championships in his stride. He then turned his attention to racing on the road, mostly in hill-climbs, with the midget car and later on with an early 500 c.c. Mark IV Cooper.

In 1953 Brabham had a real stroke of luck. At that time racing cars in Australia were extremely hard to come by and decidedly expensive, however someone had imported a new Cooper-Bristol, but before it arrived "down under" its owner departed from this world. Brabham with some financial help from the Redex oil company and his father, was fortunate enough to put in a bid that secured it.

*Formidable team. Jack looks serious as he waits for the start of a Goodwood race with "the Coopers", father and son. Charles (father) is on the left and John wears the incredible hat*

*Besides being a brilliant driver, Jack is a most proficient engineer. When his Cooper's fuel pump packed up in this year's British Empire Trophy he quickly jury-rigged a "lung-pump". Here he circulates Oulton Park with rubber fuel pipe in mouth*

*Like Fangio, Jack prefers Grand Prix machinery to sports cars, but he can drive either type good and fast. He took second place in the 2-litre class at Aintree on 18th April with this Cooper Monaco with Coventry-Climax engine*

*Typical action picture of Brabham in a Cooper-Climax single-seater. He is cornering tremendously fast in a controlled drift and he contrives to keep himself almost out of sight to reduce frontal area to a minimum*

This car really started him on the road to success, it also enabled him to compete on fairly equal terms with visiting drivers from Europe, including Bira, Whitehead, Gaze and others. From them he gained first-hand knowledge of the more attractive racing possibilities in Europe for the professional driver.

Eventually he decided he must go to England just for one season and whilst over here visit some of the leading car factories, but the fascination of motor racing in Europe still has Jack in his clutches and only occasionally is he able to return to Australia for a brief spell, usually when there is some motor racing on.

A typical example of Brabham's sportsmanship was the help he gave to Stirling Moss recently just before the final of the New Zealand Grand Prix. One of the suspension units of Stirling's Cooper had broken, Jack had the only spares and without waiting to be asked, offered them to Stirling Moss; by doing so he robbed himself of a certain win.

When he first raced in England his cornering technique was most unusual, in fact it was legacy from his midget car racing days. He got round quickly enough "by using full lock and loads of throttle", as he puts it. Nowadays he has developed a neater style and is very much faster, quick enough to take lap records at Goodwood, Crystal Palace and Brands Hatch—and victories at Silverstone and Monaco.

Third man in the Cooper team this year is Bruce McLaren from New Zealand, who is really a sort of protege of Brabham's. Under Jack's training he is coming along very quickly.

Jack has certainly come a long way during three and a half years motor racing in Europe and must be rated as a serious contender for the World Championship. ★

# JACK BRABHAM

## *potential world champion ....*

For an Australian to become a leading works driver overseas is no mean achievement, and for him to commence the 1959 season with a lead in the hotly contested Drivers Championship of the World is a triumph in itself, no matter who eventually wins the premier award.

While every Australian enthusiast is obviously applauding Jack Brabham's achievements and keeping his fingers crossed for the rest of the 1959 Grandes Epreuves, this success was forecast by one of the world's most critical motor mechanics two years ago. In his autobiography, Alf Francis wrote "Jack Brabham is that unusual combination of a first class engineer and a first class driver, so rarely found in racing." He added that Brabham "will become very much a force to be reckoned with."

Born and bred in Sydney, Jack is rather reserved, behind his unusual infectious grin.

His first experience of gas cars was at a speedway meeting which he watched in Brisbane in 1946. In an article in England, Jack said "Quite frankly, the sight frightened me to death."

Together with an American resident in Australia, Johnny Schonberg who was keen on speedway, Jack decided to build a speedway car, Johnny was to drive, while Jack would be the mechanic.

Based on a 1000 c.c. J.A.P. motor cycle engine, the car went and went well. When the time came to drive the car, it was Brabham who took the wheel and within twelve months, had won the Australian Speedway Championship at the age of 22.

Midget racing is a hard school and the experience gained between 1947 and 1951 stood Jack in good stead when he turned legitimate. But before that occurred, he took the Australian and South Australian Speedcar championships in 1949 and was South Australian Champion for the 1950-51 season.

In 1951, Jack decided to try his hand at motor sport and his first drive was at Hawesbury hillclimb in the midget car. Clipping two seconds off the hill record, and gaining FTD, Jack was disqualified when scrutineers revealed the car had only two wheel brakes.

At the Australian Hillclimb Championship held at Rob Roy in 1951, Jack won the Championship and set a new Under 1,500 c.c. class record with a time of 27.24 secs. This was the same car which had been designed 5 years before, had undergone constant modification and speedway competition, and which, with four wheel brakes and new gear ratios, left everything else for dead on its first two appearances.

Realising that despite its initial successes, a speedway car was hardly suited to the more varied rigours of motor sport, Jack bought a Cooper Mk IV, quite a rare piece of machinery at that time. In its first race, the engine blew up and while it took 18 months to return from repairs in England, Jack built up his own motor which also blew up. This was followed by a bored out ex-motor cycle H.R.D. which also gave trouble as the output was raised. Fortunately for Jack, his father had a workshop capable of handling almost any mechanical emergency. Finally a Vincent twin was modified and Brabham began competing in November 1952 at the N.S.W. Championship Hillclimb held at Newcastle. Although fastest during a wet practice, Brabham was placed third against Ron Taurenac and Dick Cobden in the final.

During following months, Brabham began to appear regularly, particularly at Mt. Druitt, and was finding that motor racing in Australia was actually making him a small profit.

In 1953, Jack won the Redex Point Score Trophy at Mt. Druitt and was then aware that he needed a more potent car.

Lacking finance to import an overseas car, Brabham was fortunate in buying the Formula 2 Cooper Bristol which David Chambers had ordered but had never received due to his untimely demise. With the aid of Redex (Aust.) Pty. Ltd., Brabham bought the car and raced it as the Redex Special under the sponsorship of this firm who, at that time, had just inaugurated the first Round Australia Trial.

With this backing, Jack was able to devote most of his time to motor sport and following a patchy start with intermittent engine troubles, he began a long succession of victories with the 1953 Queensland Road Racing Championship. He failed to run in the Australian G.P. that year after bearing failure in practice and pit errors missed him victory at Orange the same season At Ardmore, a blown gasket put him into 6th place in the First New Zealand International G.P. which Stan Jones won in the Maybach, but on his return to Sydney, a complete engine rebuild by himself and Frank Ashby produced an almost unbeatable car.

During the next season, Jack became very popular with Mount Druitt regulars, and people used to look forward eagerly to renewals of his clashes with Dick Cobden the Ferrari. Between them, they knocked the lap record down to 1.38, which nobody else has yet been able to approach. Apart from this he did well at other circuits, including Altona in particular, Fishermen's Bend, Bathhurst, Parramatta Park and Orange and came fourth in the second New Zealand Grand Prix. A few weeks afterwards, he achieved near-immortality at Orange, leading the Ferraris of Whitehead and Gaze for some laps and staying on Whitehead's tail for the rest of the race. Once again the Australian G.P., at Southport, seemed jinxed. A key in the timing gear sheared in practice. Jack and his boys worked all night mending the engine, only to have the new key shear after less than two laps of the race.

Following the row with C.A.M.S. over the advertising of Redex and the decision (now rescinded) that there could be no financial or other help to drivers in the supply of spares or equipment, Jack decided to go to England for a season.

Selling the car to Stan Jones who in turn sold it to Tom Hawkes, who converted it to the Repco Cooper, Jack left for overseas, arranging to buy Peter Whitehead's Cooper Alta. This car, although good, had seen better days and Jack later regretted not bringing over his own car.

In his first race overseas, at Goodwood, Brabham gained fourth place but at Ibsley, a week or so later, the Alta blew up.

Negotiating with John Cooper for another car, the result was a suggestion that Jack should go to the works and help construct the car. In this rear engined machine, initially bored out to 2.4 litres but later reverting to 1,971 c.c., Jack Brabham earned the distinction of being the last British car to remain running in the 1955 British G.P. at Aintree, retiring at 40 laps with engine trouble while Moss went on to win from Fangio, both driving the fabulous Mercedes Benz.

Later, in the Redex Trophy at Snetterton, Brabham led Stirling Moss until 3 laps from the end when the maestro made one of his "efforts" and forges past Brabham to win by a short lead.

Returning to Australia Jack Brabham entered the new Cooper in the Australian Grand Prix at Port Wakefield where the car performed admirably and won against much larger machines.

At Orange. in the South Pacific Championship it was again a race between Brabham and Peter Whitehead (Ferrari) with the latter again achieving victory, but with Tony Gaze also in a Ferrari running third.

By this time, Brabham had decided to go overseas permantly. Selling the Cooper Bristol to Reg Smith, he left for England with his wife Betty and son, Geoffrey in 1956. For part of his previous season, Jack had joined Tony Gaze and Tom Sulman in the Kangaroo team, but this time he was invited to become a works driver for John Cooper.

With 1956 being a rather confused European season, Brabham's racing was limited although he drove the first disc braked Cooper F2 and a Maserati.

Returning to Australia for the 1956 Australian G.P. at Albert Park, he was faced with Moss, Behra, Whitehead, Gaze and Wharton, and driving the Cooper as a sports car, did not do very well either here or in New Zealand.

Back again in England, Brabham learnt that Cooper's had entered their Formular 2 racing machines in several Grandes Epreuves. Driving as number two to Roy Salvadori, both Cooper drivers began to score an increasing number of successes.

Soon the engines were stroked to give 1,900 c.c. following development by the Rob Walker Equips and the Cooper factory. It was in this car that Jack hit world headlines.

Driving in the G.P. de Monaco, Brabham, following the triple crash of Moss, Collins and Hawthorn, found himself lying fourth behind Fangio (Maserati), Brooks (Vanwall), and von Tripps (Ferrari).

By the hundredth lap, Brabham was lying third behind Fangio and Brooks and had only five laps to go. In this fifth lap from the end, the fuel pump failed, but Brabham pushed the car to the finish, being passed during the "hike" by Maston Gregory, Lewis-Evans and Trintignant, but still gaining sixth outright placing and the applause of world press for his gallant determination.

At Aintree, Brabham was placed seventh after clutch failure had slowed him considerably, again in the Rob Walker 1.9 litre car. Throughtout this season, Brabham was plagued by mechanical trouble and was outclassed in his small car against very heavy opposition. But he was constantly gaining experience and on several occasions, bettered Salvadori's lap times.

In Formula II, the story was different and whenever Cooper works cars were running, either Brabham or Salvadori was the winner. In sports cars, he joined Raby to drive an 1,100 c.c. Cooper Climax at Le Mans to finish 15th in the general classification.

At Nurburgring, he drove the Testa Rossa Ferrari, but was reported not to have felt too comfortable.

At Goodwood, in the Formular 2 Cooper, he had set a new Formular 2 lap record which was only 0.43 sec. slower than the circuit record held by Vanwall.

To end the year, he won the 140 mile Oulton Park F2 Gold Cup Race and followed this with victory at Ardmore in an oversize twin-cam Cooper Climax.

When 1958 contracts were announced, Brabham again hit headlines by being appointed a sports car driver for Aston Martin as well as racing car driver for Coopers.

In 1958, following victory at Orange, he came fifth at Silverstone, and was only 2.2 seconds behind Modd at Aintree.

At Monaco, Jack came fourth after losing two laps checking an anti-roll bar. As co-driver with Stirling Moss, Jack Brabham was in the winning Aston Martin DBR7/300 which triumphed in the 1000 kilo. sports car race at Nurburgring.

Brabham did not get a drive at "Le Mans as Moss retired early in th race.

At Zandvoort, Brabham could not better 8th and he had to retire at Spa. In the French G.P. Brabham came 6th and again gained sixth place at Aintree in the British G.P.

Portugal saw Jack in seventh placing but was followed by a further duel with Moss at Brands Hatch in the Kentish 100 which Moss win by a short head.

This year, Jack's success began well with his first Grand Epreuve win in the first event of the International Season at Monaco to consolidate he points lead with a second placing at Zandvoort in the Dutch G.P.

Brabham's future is in the lap of the Gods, but if his luck holds, he could fulfill the prediction made by Gregor Grant in an Editorial in Autosport following Jack's winning the Autocar Formular 2 trophy in 1958. Grant wrote "Brabham has learnt a lot these past few months and could quite easily be the first Australian to win a world title."

His performances this year are being followed by many Australians not otherwise interested in motor sport.

As our most promising and most successful ambassador at large, it is perhaps fitting to conclude with the hope that Jack's luck will last the season. If it does, Brabham will prove conclusively in motor sport, as Sedhman and Hoad did in Tenis, as Landy and Elliott proved in athletics and as many other men and women have shown, that Australians have the ability to top the world in every field of sport.

# *MOTOR RACING* TRACK TEST

# FORMULA 3 REPCO BRABH

LEFT: Wim Hendriks explains the workings of his Variomatic transmission to a party of waiting test drivers at Zolder

RIGHT: The transmission mated to a Cosworth - Ford F3 power unit. The Brabham's chassis is $2\frac{1}{2}$ inches longer than standard in wheelbase, and the engine is mounted 4 inches further forward than normal.

I can now truthfully report that I have driven an F3 car through a 30 mph hairpin in the wet with 8,000 rpm on the clock, and that I kept it on the island! And just in case this starts Brabham, Chapman and Co rushing across with 'name your fee' contracts, let me hasten to add that all the credit should go to Wim Hendriks, the man who designed and developed the Variomatic transmission for the DAF passenger cars, and who has now successfully applied it to Formula 3 racing cars.

The story really starts back in 1964, when Hendriks was given the go-ahead to fit a Variomatic transmission unit into an Alexis chassis, with a view to publicising the reliability and efficiency of the system, and to remove any doubts in the minds of new-car buyers as to the practicality of belt drive.

The Variomatic Alexis was given its first outings by Rob Slotemaker, who finished seventh overall in the F3 race preceding the Monaco Grand Prix in 1965, and was then handed over to Jack Brabham to test. Though somewhat shattered by the car's reluctance to go where he pointed it, Jack was sufficiently impressed with the transmission to agree to modify an existing F3 Repco Brabham chassis to accommodate it. Since then, two more chassis have been built, $2\frac{1}{2}$ inches longer than standard in wheelbase, and with the Cosworth-Ford engine moved 4 inches further forward. As most people will know, some very heartening results were achieved last season in conjunction with the Chequered Flag, who entered the DAF-transmission car, and with Mike Beckwith, who did most of the driving.

The high spot of the season was at Zolder, in September, when in very good company Beckwith finished first in one race and third in two more, and DAF are now convinced that they have something worthwhile to offer racing, apart from any publicity rub-off which their participation in it may give them. For 1967, a two-car team is being operated on their behalf by the Chequered Flag, with Mike Beckwith and that very promising young Dutchman Gijs van Lennep as regular drivers.

Track testing the Repco Brabham-DAF meant a break from the Brands Hatch tradition, and a trip over to Zolder, just on the Belgian side of the border with Holland, and conveniently close to the DAF headquarters at Eindhoven. Roughly $2\frac{1}{2}$ miles round, it has something of the flavour of both the Nurburgring and Zandvoort, with a potential lap time of 1m 41s for a Formula 3 car in the dry. With brilliant timing, the first spots of rain fell just before I climbed in, and the track became wetter and wetter as the day progressed until even van Lennep was barely hitting the 2 minute barrier. Fortunately, that was the only thing we hit all day, although the four of us who drove the car amassed a fair number of spins!

For anyone unfamiliar with the Variomatic system provided on DAF passenger cars, the gearing provided by the twin belts running in variable-diameter pulleys is influenced by a system of bobweights acting on the primary pulleys, with a supplementary variation in ratio being achieved by manifold pressure or a vacuum operating on a diaphragm adjacent to the pulleys.

The transmission requirements on the race track, of course, are very different from those on the road, mainly because in racing (and in particular when racing with small-capacity, high-revving engines) you use only a small percentage of the available rev range, and cannot afford any time lag while the revs climb up to an effective level after a period on over-run.

The manifold-influenced diaphragm, therefore, has been replaced by an ingenious device which ensures that the gearing is automatically lowered immediately the engine goes on to over-run, and in this way the revs are kept to a minimum of around 7,500 rpm, even when coming into the slowest corner.

The device consists of a peg which engages in a spiral groove cut out of the wall of a cylindrical cage mounted on the axis of the front pulleys. The peg itself, mounted outboard of the left-hand pulley, is driven by the hollow countershaft, but the cage merely floats on the outside of the countershaft, and is coupled in turn to a thin rod running inside the shaft, and that is connected to the outside surface of the pulley on the other side of the car.

With the engine driving the car at maximum speed, the peg is hard up against one end of the groove, while the cage has floated away from the adjacent pulley, and by means of the thin rod has also pulled the faces of the offside pulley together to give the highest possible gearing. But immediately the engine backs off, the countershaft will have the effect of braking the peg's motion while the cylindrical cage continues to revolve at its former speed. This causes the peg to move along the spiral groove, the cage to move inwards, the pulley faces to part, and the gearing to drop.

A centrifugal clutch, encased in a steel-lined aluminium housing, transmits the drive from the crankshaft to bevel gears on the primary countershaft by means of three spring-controlled shoes, the spring tension being sufficient to delay engagement until approximately 5,500 rpm instead of around 1,000 rpm on the DAF 44 saloon. The springs are supported by dowels to prevent them breaking loose at high speed.

On an earlier installation, the primary countershaft was placed behind the secondary shaft, resulting in a rather tail-heavy chassis, while overall gearing was adjusted by means of drop gears on the output shaft. On the latest and most successful application, however, the primary shaft is ahead of, and the secondary shaft immediately behind, the final-drive line, and a train of three gears runs forward from the secondary shaft to the differential to establish the overall gearing. The primary shaft gear reduction is 2.54 to 1, and with a 3.25 to 1 differential (3.46 and 3.70 diffs are also available), overall gearing can be varied between 5.33 and 17.20 to 1. Weight distribution, with driver, is 45/55 per cent front to

# No. 59 by John Blunsden

## AM-DAF

rear with the latest transmission layout.

Climbing aboard, the first unusual feature you see is the matching pair of rev counters. One, in fact, acts as a speedometer (after appropriate conversion), and is used to establish overall gearing requirements on new circuits. It is not used during racing, and had been disconnected before the test. The conventional gear shift has been replaced by a simple right-handed push-pull lever, giving neutral or drive, with a spring-loaded flap beneath guarding a further movement backwards to get reverse.

Lifting the front body section reveals a two-in-one brake pedal, the conventional clutch pedal having been coupled to the brake to offer either right or left-foot braking. By the time I had slipped right down in the cockpit I found that my right leg was bent too much to get to the brake pedal comfortably, and so I used my left leg and the left pedal throughout the test. Gijs van Lennep, incidentally, is convinced that left-foot braking is the answer for both speed and accuracy.

Wet-track starts are usually tricky, but with Variomatic there is no drama at all. It virtually eliminates wheelspin on the most slippery of surfaces, and you can floor the accelerator and accelerate smoothly ahead while all the boys with conventional transmissions are anxiously watching their rev counters and correcting their slides. For a racing start, the technique seems to be to hold the engine at around 5,000 rpm until a second or two before flag-fall, then build it up to 6,000 or 6,500 rpm, holding the car back on the footbrake, then simultaneously lift one foot and drop the other as the flag comes down.

The first few laps were spent in finding out where the corners went. The wide pit straight narrows down into a tight 90-degree left-hander, followed by a short straight leading into a double-right-hander needing two distinct stabs and adding up to about 180 degrees (very weird, that one!). Another short straight alongside a canal leads into a third right-hander and on to the main straight, parallel to, and behind, the pits. A fast left-hand curve leads uphill beneath a pedestrian bridge and over a sharp blind hump where the car feels as though it gets airborne but doesn't quite.

In the dry the 'stars' take this flat-out in top, building up speed down the other side and through the left-hander at the foot of the incline before braking for a slowish right-hander. Almost immediately comes another right-hander, then a left curve followed by a drop down to the right-handed hairpin (and a gate barring the escape road!). The up-hill run back to the pits straight is punctuated by two left-handed 'S' bends, the first of which can be straight-lined, and the second taken just about flat, I should think, in the dry.

The first lap or two seemed very strange, and I never realised quite to what extent you rely upon your ears when driving. The most

**Mike Beckwith giving one of the Chequered Flag cars a run. The longer-than-usual wheelbase is evident from this picture, while the belt pulleys are clearly visible at the rear.**

difficult thing is to judge your approach speed into corners with the engine revving away behind you, and inevitably you err on the slow side. It takes time, but you have to almost completely disregard what you hear and try to concentrate on the car's feel as you sort out braking points.

The size of the bobweights had been adjusted on this car to allow a peak crankshaft speed of 9,200 rpm, but 9,000 rpm comes up very soon after leaving a corner with the power full on. It took the length of the back straight to collect those last 200 revs, and as you wait for

**The cage and peg device which ensures that the gearing is lowered automatically as the engine goes onto over-run. The countershaft-mounted peg runs along the spiral groove, forcing the pulley faces apart and causing the gearing to drop as the driver lifts off.**

the speed to rise with an almost constant engine note in the background, the power limitations imposed by Formula 3 regulations are brought into very clear focus. I hasten to add that, as lap times have proved, the DAF-transmission car accelerates just as quickly (or slowly!) as an equivalent F3 car with a four-speed gearbox.

In view of the constant high revs, I expected the water temperature to be on the high side, but on this admittedly very cold day the engine ran over-cool if anything. The brakes were the weakest part of the car. There was ample stopping power for the wet conditions, but heavy braking produced considerable front-end patter, inducing intermittent wheel lock, and there would seem to be a need for stronger uprights on this particular machine.

The handling performance of a well-sorted F3 Repco Brabham is a byword, and as far as one could tell in these really diabolical conditions, the installation of the DAF transmission had further increased the safety factor. With no sudden changes in torque, traction seemed to be unusually good, particularly over the rougher sections of the course—and there are quite a few of those! On the other hand, subtle variations in engine note can tell you quite a lot about what the rear wheels of a racing car are doing, and these of course are missing from a DAF-transmission one. I spun it at the hairpin on one lap, I believe because I had been lulled into a false sense of security by the constant engine note, and consequently was just that fraction of a second too slow in correcting the slide when the rear wheels let go. Mind you, with a river across the track at that point I should have been ready for anything!

With a busy race season already behind it, the car was subjected to a very full day of testing at Zolder, during which it suffered nothing worse than a faulty plug and a leaking oil union, causing the belts to be sprayed with lubricant, which in turn had the effect of intermittently increasing the maximum revs to around 9,600 rpm until the belts had dried out. Although belts are normally changed after two races, this is purely a precaution because they will in fact last very much longer—the first signs of wear are when the internal notches develop knife cuts.

Clutch wear is indicated by the take-up speed of the transmission—if the drive is not transmitted below 6,500 rpm the clutch is stripped and replaced. In order to conserve the clutch as much as possible the cars are not driven at slow speed in the paddock, but are wheeled out on to the track (there's not many places in the average race paddock where you can do 5,500 rpm or more, even in your lowest gear!).

By 1968, says DAF's amiable competitions manager, Rob Koch, the company hope to be in a position to supply a limited number of Variomatic transmission kits to Jack Brabham as an alternative to four-speed gearboxes for his Formula 3 'production' cars, and for about the same price. From what I have sampled, and from what the coming season promises from the two team cars, I reckon Jack could well have a queue for them by then.

# THE CHAMPION'S CAR

**L. J. K. Setright reviews the design and development of the 3 litre Repco Brabham BT24, most successful Formula I car of 1967 and star of the Autospeed '68 Exhibition**

**RATHER more than a century ago, there came an impassioned call from Thoreau:** *Our life is frittered away by detail . . . simplify, simplify!* **Rather more than a year ago, there was an equally impassioned cry going up from the majority of racing car constructors engaged in Formula I:** *What has the Brabham got that we haven't?* **The answer to their question was simple: Nothing—in fact, it has rather less, but rather differently arranged.**

The new generation of Formula I cars contesting Grands Prix under the 3 litre formula that began in 1966 tended towards elaboration and complexity. The Honda had its 12 cylinders curiously clustered in threes to permit power to be abstracted from the middle of a roller-bearing crankshaft; the BRM had its 16 cylinders disposed in a horizontal H formation involving two crankshafts; the Gurney-Weslake V12 contained 48 valves; and they all went a lot slower than they should have done. But whereas there were several elaborate details in these cars that, in the light of subsequent events, wanted justification, there was none in the Repco Brabham that was superfluous; and it went faster than it should have done.

As in 1966 so in 1967 the story has continued. Before each race the pundits could be heard discussing form: 'Provided that the Weslake engine and the Lotus chassis display their usual want of reliability, the Brabham should win'. There was seldom any question of the Brabham breaking. Indeed, there were occasions when an outright unqualified declaration of confidence in the Brabham could be heard, as before the French Grand Prix on that miserably inadequate Bugatti circuit at Le Mans.

Nor must we give the impression that the Brabham was merely an habitual survivor though not as fast as its rivals. Other cars came and went during the course of 1966, but of those that campaigned throughout the season, only the 3 litre Ferrari was consistently and demonstrably faster, by a margin of about 0.7 per cent. Of course, the Brabham won more races—indeed, it finished more races—and long before the season was over, the Brabham was confirmed in the Championship lists as the most successful car of the year. It was not otherwise in 1967, although there was no doubt that the Lotus 49 and Ferrari were faster than, and the Eagle as fast as, the Brabham. Perhaps recent history can be too often retold, and it is hardly necessary here to recapitulate the series of fastest laps and high placings or outright wins credited to Messrs Hulme and Brabham during the course of the year. But although the cars were sufficiently similar in detail, there was enough difference in the manifestations of '66 and '67 to justify a re-examination of the engineering behind the names. Whereas in 1966 the World Champion Driver was Brabham and the World Champion Constructor was Brabham so that we tended to concentrate perhaps on Brabham the man, this year the World Champion Driver was Hulme, and therefore we must concentrate on Brabham the car; at which point it is meet to remind ourselves that the car is not a Brabham, but a Repco Brabham.

In the early months of 1966 it was easy to dismiss the Repco contribution, the 3 litre V8, as nothing more than a half-hearted approximation to a racing engine. We soon learned that we were doing it less than justice: it might be an engine that was an exception to many of the rules, but it was undeniably effective and successful.

To be sure, the Repco engine was not at all powerful for its day and age. For an unsupercharged 3 litre engine running on petrol to generate a mere 300 bhp would have been thought not immoderate in the previous decade, when the petrol-burning $2\frac{1}{2}$-litre Vanwall developed 262, and the BRM 275; and the fact that the latter could, despite its four big cylinders, turn comfortably at 8,500 rpm to develop its maximum power, made the placard speed of the eight cylinder Repco seem something of a handicap at 8,200 rpm.

However, the engine was notably light in weight, scaling a mere 340 lbs, had a very satisfactory torque curve, and featured a stroke/bore ratio that, at 0.68:1, was lower than that of any Grand Prix engine other than the V8 Coventry Climax $1\frac{1}{2}$ litre motor which, in its final 1965 form, got down to 0.63:1. This turns out on examination to be a most important feature.

By what combination of luck and good judgment the Repco engineers (headed by Phil Irving) arrived at these full-bellied cylinders is not exactly clear, but it is not improbable that the convenience factor influenced their choice of basic design—the Oldsmobile $3\frac{1}{2}$ litre V8 that General Motors had discontinued a couple of years earlier. Little more than the main crankcase-cum-cylinder-block casting was to be retained in the 1966 engine, but this was sufficient to determine its proportions. To reduce the cylinder bore would be misguided; to reduce the piston stroke was therefore natural; and if, in consequence, the cylinder head face was rather a long way from the crankthrow, then to minimise piston weight and use abnormally long connecting rods was commonsense. Yet it was from this logical sequence of adaptations that the virtues of the Repco engine stemmed.

The advantages of a short stroke in relation to cylinder bore are sufficiently well known to need little review here. The amplitude of piston area resultant from such an arrangement may in itself be desirable, but less so than the consequent provision of space for valves of very large diameter, thus making it possible to inspire and exhale the greatest quantity of air to be burned within the cylinders. There are some disadvantages, which many engine designers held to be of some importance, although they had been somewhat overtaken by events. One was the difficulty of arranging a combustion chamber of satisfactory shape while still providing a desirably high compression ratio; but this was to some extent played down by the change of regulations that came into effect in 1958, requiring Formula I cars to consume petrol instead of allowing them freedom to run on any fuel. The lower compression ratios possible with petrol, compared with what can usefully be employed when alcohol is burned, gave designers considerable scope for reducing stroke/bore ratios, as they did in the early 1960s; and in any case it was being more generally recognised by then that there is more power to be gained by designing for valve area than by designing for compression ratio.

There were other mechanical objections to a squat pot. If the piston diameter be appreciably larger or smaller than its stroke, then it is necessary to apply what has been christened the Lanchester correction. As long ago as 1905 Dr Frederick Lanchester demonstrated that one must divide the piston speed by the square root of the ratio of stroke to bore in order to get a true measure of the internal stresses. Otherwise the short-stroke engine would suffer a level of mechanical stress somewhat higher than might appear on paper, and might be expected to prove unreliable. Had this theory been commonly adopted by racing engine designers, stroke/bore ratios might not have been expected to drop to fractions appreciably below unity unless this were accompanied by a proportionate increase in the length of connecting rods in order to minimise the acceleration of the piston and its rings. In fact, the stroke/bore ratio dropped considerably over the years from 1954 to 1966: it did so without the accompanying stretching of con rods, and to a degree that can be shown to have a direct relationship to the development of the maximum power from an engine of limited capacity. In 1954, racing engines of GP calibre had a stroke/bore ratio of about 0.9:1; by the end of 1965 they had dropped to a mere 0.7:1. During the interval, brake mean effective pressures had not altered significantly, and with all other factors remaining static it must be significant that engine efficiency in terms of power per litre has on the average risen in precisely the same proportion as the stroke/bore ratio has dropped. Incidentally, a representative figure for peak engine speed in 1954 would bear the same mathematical relationship to an equally representative figure for 1965.

The fact remains that Dr Lanchester's calculations show mechanical stresses to be intimately related to stroke/bore ratio, which is why so many engine designers have been tempted by a multiplicity of cylinders. Repco circumvented the only unsatisfactory chamber in the cylinder head should be wedge-shaped rather than bearing any relation whatever to the classical hemisphere, especially since this made it possible to incline the valves and the whole train of valve gear at an angle of 10° inboard from the piston axis, and thus make it just possible to get the engine into the chassis for which it was intended. Anyway, the nature of the combustion chamber cannot have hampered the Repco engine, for if the peak bhp (which was *not* the principal object of the exercise) was only 300 or so at 8,000 rpm, peak torque (which *was*) amounted to 230 lbs/ft at 6,500 rpm, equivalent to a bmep of 192 lbs/in²—which can be compared with the 195 of the little Coventry-Climax V8 with which Clark and Lotus won the 1965 Championships. Moreover, although the peak of the bmep and torque curves occurred at 6,500 rpm, real power was forthcoming from rates as low as 4,000, making life much easier for the drivers.

Not only was the Repco engine a paragon of tractability, but it also carried away the palm in lightness. With a weight to power ratio of 1.13 lb/bhp it was even better than the V6 Ferrari (1.18 lb/bhp) and the 2½ litre Coventry Climax (1.22) that had hitherto seemed of such exceptional merit. The Repco's weight of 340 lbs compared more than interestingly with the 420 of the H16 BRM or the 435 of the W196 Mercedes-Benz.

Lightness was clearly of the essence as far as the Repco and Brabham design teams were concerned. Throughout 1966 and for the early part of 1967 the Repco Brabham was generally regarded as the lightest 3 litre car in Formula I racing, although in the earlier year it still weighed 150 lbs more than the 1,102 minimum that the regulations permit. The two cars in which Brabham and Hulme campaigned in 1966 were quite different in many chassis details, the BT20 which was the later of the two having a frame that weighed a mere 70 lbs. Further paring and pruning led to this year's car, the BT24, being even more compact, its proportions closely akin to those of a Formula 2 car.

The 1967 car has nevertheless been the typical idiosyncratic Brabham spaceframe, a confection of welded tubing now unique in an age of stressed skin hulls. If we were to ask of the designer, Ron Tauranac, not *how does he do it?* but rather *why does he do it?* perhaps it would become less fashionable to decry the means by which the Brabham team as a whole achieve such notable ends.

Of course the tubular spaceframe chassis represents only a halfway stage in the elimination of structural imperfections. Of course a stressed-skin hull, a monocoque if you are lucky, should be lighter and stiffer. Of course; but it is not all that much lighter, the additional stiffness is of debatable value, and associated snags make the stressed-skin hull often more of a liability than an asset. The spaceframe is easy to repair, easy to replace. If you want to change the mounting point of a suspension element, you can do it easily in a spaceframe, whereas to do it in a shell frame involves at least the skilful addition of local stiffening and ideally entire redesign of the structure. Fuel tanks may well be an integral part of the stressed-skin hull instead of being appendages to a spaceframe, but in the former case they then have to be made in a much more substantial way, and are not necessarily any easier to accommodate, so the difference in weight is negligible. The difference in convenience is undeniable: you could build, develop and modify three or four multi-tubular cars in the time you would need to make the press tools for a monocoque prototype.

All right, these arguments are well known and largely accepted by those to whom expediency is more prized than rectitude. The fact remains that the stressed-skin hull is much stiffer than the spaceframe, and yet here is Setright saying that this could be a bad thing. Is this not rank heresy?

Were racing cars even nearly perfect,

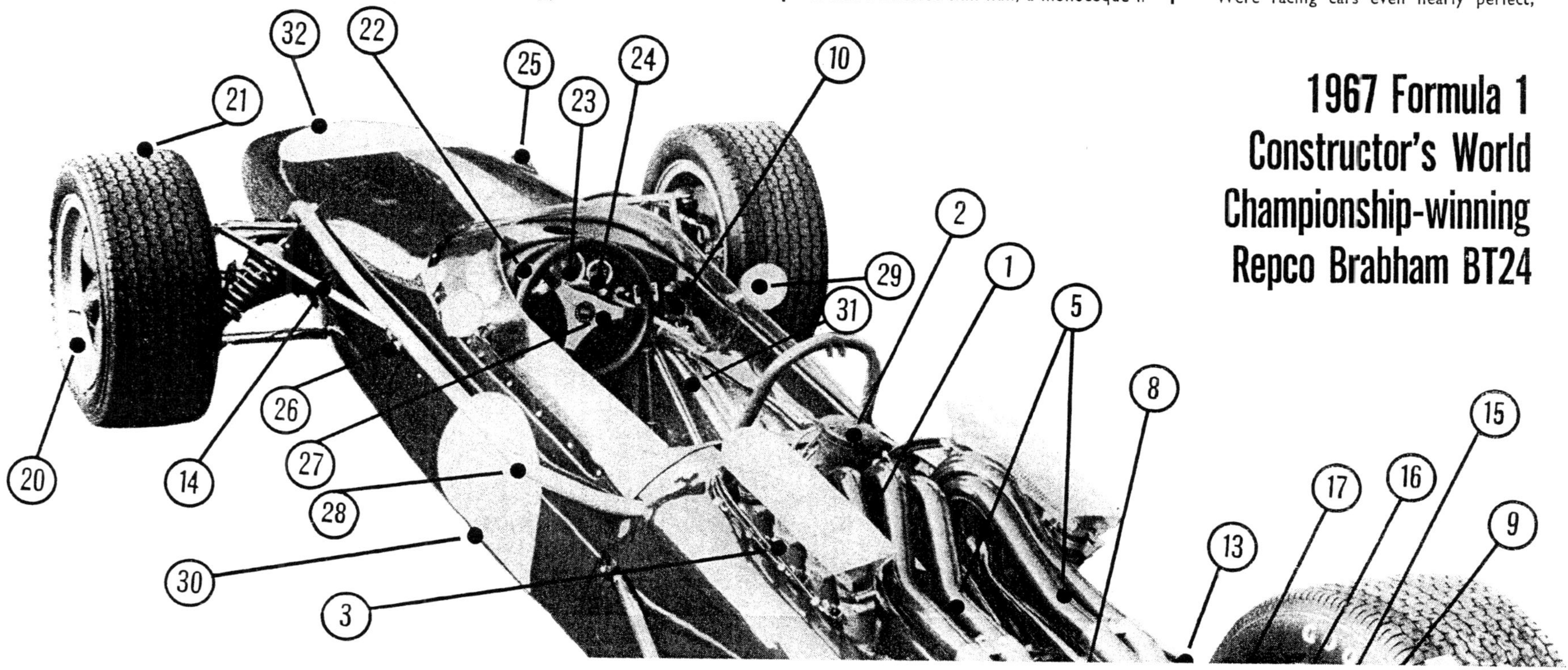


**1967 Formula 1 Constructor's World Championship-winning Repco Brabham BT24**

implications of an ultra-short stroke/bore ratio by making use of connecting rods whose length between centres was three times that of the stroke, instead of that of the conventional two times: in this way piston accelerations and constant inertia loadings were substantially reduced, and side thrust on the pistons was also lessened.

The connecting rods came from the production $4\frac{1}{2}$ litre V8 Daimler, and were therefore cheap and expendable, just as was the Oldsmobile crankcase casting. It may be that the mechanical limitations of such standard components as these were largely responsible for the rather limited rotational speed of the Repco engine; but while a high rate of revolutions is necessary to the generation of great power, engine speed does not really figure in the development of the utmost torque. This was the star to which Repco and Brabham hitched their wagon: there had been enough examples in the past of frenetically powerful engines proving inadequate in competition with less powerful but more flexible engines, especially when the latter were often put in cars that could be made lighter and simpler. And this is precisely the recipe for the Repco Brabham—lightness, simplicity and an ample spread of torque.

Here again the short stroke and therefore tremendous piston area became relevant. The Repco engine was remarkable for having only one overhead camshaft per bank of cylinders, and for having its valves mounted in line and parallel rather than inclined in opposition to each other at an included angle of anything from 50 to 100°, as had hitherto been universal. It followed naturally from this valve layout that the combustion

## KEY TO NUMBERED COMPONENTS

1—Repco type 740 90 degree V8 3 litre engine.
2—Distributor for Bosch ignition.
3—Lucas fuel injector nozzles upstream of throttle slide.
4—High pressure Lucas electric fuel pump with heat shield from gearbox.
5—Separate exhaust clusters for each cylinder bank, because of single-plane crankshaft.
6—Lukey Muffler exhaust megaphones.
7—Hewland DG300 five-speed gearbox.
8—Housing of ZF limited-slip differential.
9—Plastic catch-tank for oil breathers—originally a screen washer bottle.
10—Right-hand gear-change lever operating through rod linkage.
11—Spigotted rubber doughnut for plunge—lighter and cheaper than splines, and no danger of binding under power.
12—Hooke joint for drive-shaft articulation.
13—Upper of two long parallel radius arms, pair on each side, to take braking and acceleration rear suspension loads into chassis and give vertical rear upright bump movement.
14—Rear strut of top front wishbone extended aft to take braking loads in tension, feeding them and normal suspension loads into tubular 'bulkhead' at scuttle. Bottom wishbone is extended forward for similar reasons.
15—11 inch diameter rear disc brakes, $\frac{3}{8}$ inch thick. Similar units at front are 12 inches in diameter by $\frac{7}{16}$ inch thick.
16—Girling brake calipers, at rear, as at front, using Ferodo pads.
17—Armstrong co-axial coil spring/damper units used at front and rear.
18—MRD cast magnesium rear wheels, 12 inches x 15 inches size.
19—Goodyear 6.00/1310 x 15 inch tyres at rear.
20—MRD cast magnesium front wheels, 8 inches x 15 inches size.
21—Goodyear 4.75/1095 x 15 inch tyres at front.
22—Smiths combined fuel pressure and water temperature gauge.
23—Smiths electronic tachometer gauge.
24—Smiths combined oil temperature and oil pressure gauge.
25—Air intake to duct cool air to driver's feet.
26—Water temperature gauge pick-up point on water pipe.
27—Small diameter Formula leather-rimmed steering wheel.
28—External water pipe so placed in order to give extra water cooling and remove heat source from cockpit for hot races such as Mexico and South Africa.
29—Winkrace rear-view mirrors.
30—Specialised Mouldings-produced glass fibre body panelling.
31—Fuel tank (15 gallons) strapped to frame; another on the opposite flank.
32—Serck water and oil radiator and oil tank mounted in nose of car ahead of pedals.

perhaps it might be. But they are very far from it, as are all man's artefacts. The torsional stiffness of a Formula 1 monocoque chassis may easily amount to 2 or 3,000 lb ft/degree, or even as much as 10,000 in the case of such exceptional examples of structural engineering as the Mallite McLaren of 1966. The Repco Brabham manages about 1,000, and Mr Tauranac is happy with that. He could be right, too.

It's all a question of the relative importance of slow corners and fast ones. In the tightest hairpins such as Station Corner at Monte Carlo, a top-grade car will spend only about $1\frac{1}{2}$ seconds at its peak lateral *g* while negotiating the corner—whence it follows that the difference between cornering at *g* and at 1.4 *g* (reasonable figures by present standards) in this case would be a scant eighth of a second. On the other hand, a long sweeping curve such as those encountered at Spa, tight enough to impose considerable *g* loadings and at the same time fast enough to allow the best drivers to go through very fast, may occupy them for a good ten seconds in its negotiation. Ten seconds is an awfully long time to spend balancing steering and throttle against centrifugal force and tyre grip, especially if the car is on the brink of uncontrollability. Thus the difference between 0.9 and 1 g through a bend such as this (and again the figures are reasonable) means a difference of exactly 0.5 second in the time spent going through the bend, equivalent to perhaps 30 yards at the speeds involved. It seems to me that what Tauranac has done is to risk an eighth of a second to gain half a second.

This needs further elaboration. The

stiffness of a monocoque hull will best ensure maintenance of a precise spatial relationship between the car and its wheels upon which the generation of the highest cornering forces depends. This is of great importance in those slow tight corners where lateral accelerations are at their highest. In a really fast open bend, however, other factors come in to play, notably wheel adhesion. This depends upon the nicety with which spring rates are calculated and achieved in manufacture, so that the wheel and tyre may follow as faithfully as possible the inevitable undulations of the road surface. The slightest discrepancy in manufacture, the slightest imbalance of spring rates between one front wheel and the other, for example, and the road holding of the car is prejudiced no less surely than it would be, say, by a discrepancy in damper settings. The same trouble can be experienced when braking at high speeds, that tyre which is kept more consistently in contact with the road surface proving less liable to lock than its mate, which may be jumping up and down. All this can be masked by a chassis frame that is somewhat flexible so as to be tantamount to an inter-connecting spring, whereas the stiffness of a good monocoque may prevent it being so accommodating. Such principles can, of course, be taken to excess, but I think there is something in the theory. Lest there be those who consider this idle speculation, let me point out that the effect is observable and can be substantiated in figures. Timing cars through slow corners and through fast ones, I have found that the Brabhams are almost invariably slower than the best of their rivals through tight slow corners, but are usually faster through open high-speed bends. This applies not only in Formula I, where there are a number of variables that may mask the effects, but also in Formula 2 where, for instance, the Brabham commonly has the same engine as the Lotus.

Another notable feature of the Brabham is that it has retained a somewhat narrow track at a time when all the others are growing wider and wider. In previous issues of this magazine I have pointed out that it is possible to increase the track of a monoposto racing car without increasing the aerodynamic drag, because the increase in frontal area is very slight and is compensated by the decrease in turbulence in the gaps between wheels and fuselage. This is all very well, but the complexity of the latest suspension systems makes a large measure of turbulence unavoidable in this area; so although most manufacturers take pains to mount their front springs and dampers inboard out of the wind, they never seem to succeed in doing the same at the rear—though you would have thought that they would have tried torsion bars by now.

Top: *The front end of the guvnor's Repco Brabham just before a final test at Goodwood prior to the South African GP.* Left: *The cockpit, minus seat, showing fire extinguisher, battery, gearchange etc.* Above: *The BT24's back end.*

## General Specification

**Type BT24 3 litre Formula I car, 1967**

**Engine:** Repco Type 740 90 degree V8; 89 mm x 60 mm, 2,996 cc. Light alloy block with wet cylinder liners; chain-driven single overhead camshafts operating two vertical valves per cylinder. Single-plane, five-bearing Laystall crankshaft. Bosch distributor and coil ignition; Champion plugs; Lucas fuel injection. Power output: approx 330 bhp at 8,800 rpm.

**Transmission:** Borg and Beck twin-plate clutch; Hewland DG300 5-speed gearbox; ZF limited slip differential. Spigotted rubber 'doughnuts' and Hooke-jointed drive shafts.

**Braking:** Girling discs front and rear; Ferodo pads.

**Suspension:** Double triangulated wishbones and coil springs-cum-damper units at front; inverted lower wishbones and single upper links in conjunction with coil spring-cum-damper units and twin parallel radius arms.

**Wheels:** MRD magnesium, 8 inches x 15 inches front, 10 inches x 15 inches or 12 inches x 15 inches rear.

**Tyres:** Goodyear; 4.75/1095 x 15 inches front. 6.00/1310 x 15 inches rear.

**Dimensions:** 7 feet $9\frac{3}{4}$ inches wheelbase; 4 feet 5 inches track at front, 4 feet $7\frac{3}{4}$ inches at rear (when using 10 inches x 15 inches wheels with 6.00/1310 tyres and 5/8 inch spacers). Overall length (with tailpipes) 13 feet; overall width, 5 feet $9\frac{1}{2}$ inches; maximum body width, 2 feet $2\frac{1}{2}$ inches; height to top of roll-over hoop 2 feet $10\frac{1}{2}$ inches. Weight empty 1,102.5 lbs.

The thing that prompts car designers to widen the track is the sensitivity of modern racing tyres to variations in wheel camber; but here the idiosyncratic Brabham is at an advantage, for the Goodyear tyres that designer Bert Baldwin and his Wolverhampton craftsmen make for Brabham are blessed with more sidewall compliance than any others at present in the field. They are thus less sensitive to camber change, more progressive in their approach to the limit, and help to endow the Brabham with agility and controllability at highly competitive cornering speeds. So Mr Tauranac keeps his track narrow, keeps the frontal area down, and in the circumstances does not have to bother about shoe-horning the front springing media indoors, since they will not make a great deal of difference to the drag if left out in the cool fresh air.

All this compactness and lightness cannot entirely account for the surprising speed of the Brabham. I suspect that the power developed by the 1967 engine is considerably more than its tight-lipped proprietors seem prepared to admit. With the revision of the chassis for 1967 there was a redesign of the engine, the cheap and expendable Oldsmobile main casting being replaced by a new Repco component, allowing the adoption of entirely new cylinder heads. These still have only one camshaft each, still have their valves in line ahead and parallel. But the valves are no longer inclined to the cylinder axis, being perpendicular to the headface, suggesting that the wedge-shaped combustion chamber is no more. Precisely just what does lurk therein, we are not told. Were it other than a Heron-type combustion space in the crown of the piston, we would be surprised. That the car could only go as fast as it has done under the influence of considerably more bhp than the 335 suggested by some commentators, we are convinced.

Even so, the Brabham remains an example, like Vespasian, of how great ends can be achieved by modest means. To be sure, it has demonstrated greater reliability than could any of its 1967 rivals; but it has always been closely competitive with them while they were running, even to the extent of usually being among the leaders on the starting grid. Yet this is the car which is said to be inferior to its rivals in so many respects: it is allegedly inferior to this one in power, to that one in weight, to another in frontal area, perhaps to them all in chassis and suspension design (thought it remains the only example in which braking loads are properly distributed through the front suspension linkages and their pickup points on the chassis). All this may be true; and if it is, why, the Repco Brabham is the most inferior racing car ever to have proved itself the world's best.

# Second Win for Brabham at Levin

DRIVING his own Formula Libre car, Jack Brabham won the Vic Hudson Memorial Race at Levin on January 12 when he finished 16.3 secs ahead of Tony Maggs in a 2.7 Lola. It was the Australian's first win with the Repco-Brabham in a race which suffered heavily from suspension and transmission breakage on the tough 1.1 mile circuit. Innes Ireland finished third in the Ferguson, almost half a lap behind Jack, while the first New Zealander home was Roly Levis (Cooper) in fourth position. Thomasen was fifth in his Cooper, followed by Sager (Lotus), Young (1500 c.c. Cooper) and Flowers (1100 c.c. Gemini).

Rain fell on Friday's practice session, and times were well down on Shelly's 53 seconds lap record set last year. Ireland was finding strange happenings with the Ferguson and its unusual characteristics. Innes said that when navigating a corner and the tail of the car began to slide, he would apply opposite lock and tap the throttle—the normal procedure. But every time he did this he shot off the circuit with the Ferguson! Brabham had soon recorded the fastest lap with an official time of 55 secs, with Surtees and McLaren 56 secs each, though pit crews thought their times were slower.

Being such a tight little circuit, Levin is the scene of many exciting saloon car duels and in practice interest was centred around McLaren's 83 b.h.p. Mini Cooper and the Palmerston North driver Kerry Grant in his FJ-engined Farina A40. Bruce beat the A40 by only 0.2 secs., lapping at 64.5 secs on normal tyres after attempting to use the German SP rain tyres. Both cars defeated McBeath's hot 3.8 Jaguar by a considerable margin.

**Jolly Jack ever popular amongst Racing fans surrounded by youthful admirers after winning the 30 mile dash.**

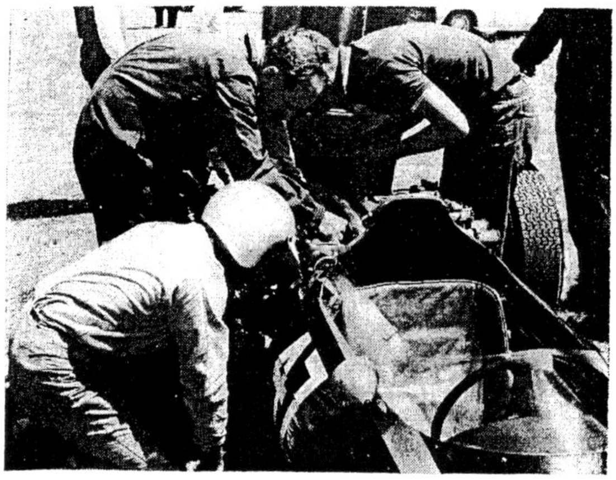

**Bruce McLaren, Harry Pearce and Wally Wilmott make a last minute inspection of the engine room of the International Cooper.**

### The Heats

Two heats were run in the morning of the big day for the 28-lap final, and Jim Palmer looked set in heat 1 in the Bowmaker 2.7 Coper when distributor trouble lost him the lead after two laps. David Young thereupon took the lead in his 1500 c.c. Cooper and ran home first followed by Ken Sager (1500 c.c. Lotus), Rex Flowers (Gemini) and Rod Coppins (Tec Mec). Ireland took the lead in the second heat which featured the absence of McLaren (broken clutch being repaired) and Tony Shelly (broken engine mount on his Lotus). Soon Brabham was past Innes, who was having gearbox ailings, on lap 4 when the two Lolas of Surtees and Maggs both retired, John suffering a broken striker lever in the gearbox and Tony with a broken left rear half shaft. Hyslop finished second after a grand battle with Amon, and Ireland was fourth.

Brabham, Hyslop, Amon and Young occupied the front row for the big race, with Ireland, Levis and Thomasen second row. McLaren, Shelly, Sager and Flowers sat in row three while the three Bowmaker cars of Surtees, Maggs and Palmer were at the back of the field. The acceleration of the Ferguson is fantastic with the four wheel drive, but Ireland had to sit in behind Brabham soon after the start, followed by Hyslop, McLaren, Amon, Maggs. Palmer and Surtees were already out on the first lap, the Englishman having gearbox trouble again, and the Hamilton driver had a broken crown wheel in the Cooper. On the fifth lap McLaren had taken Hyslop and then Ireland, setting out for the leading Brabham. Meantime Shelly was driving well on the home track, passing Hyslop, Amon and Maggs for fourth position. McLaren now reduced the lap record to 52s in and effort to catch Brabham. The order on lap 13 was Brabham, McLaren, Shelly, Ireland, Maggs, Hyslop, after the retirement of Chris Amon with magneto trouble.

### McLaren Spun

On lap 18 McLaren had closed right in on Brabham but 'tried too hard" and spun off at the Cabbage Tree loop, bending the right front suspension on a pile of tyres. Tony Maggs took Shelly on the 19th circulation for second position while Ireland was still having difficulties with the Ferguson's gearbox. One lap earlier the Australian had recorded the fastest lap, a new record, of 51.8s. Brabham now began to ease up with his 20s lead while Maggs semed content in second place, and Shelly driving probably his best race this season in third position. On lap 21 a broken half shaft put Hyslop out of the running. Shelly began to work hard again in his Lotus and passed the South African driver, but the right rear suspension upright broke just as he had taken second position. He spun in front of Maggs and very nearly came to grief as the passing Lola sheared the nose off his Lotus. Magg's Lola was unharmed and he ran in to the finish in second place, with Ireland nursing the Ferguson into third position.

The first saloon scratch race was divided into two classes, C. Hogan winning the up to 1300 c.c. class in his red Anglia with H. McLeod in a Mini second. G. Bremer (Hillman) won the over 1301 c.c. class and A. Lawrence (Peugeot) was second. The second saloon event was a crowd pleaser with Kerry Grant (A40) and Denis Marwood (Humber 80)

**The Brabham resting after winning its first race.**
**—Photo by Jack Inwood**

**Rex Flowers' Gemini losing petrol from a loose tank which was later removed and Flowers went on to take 7th place.**
**—Photo by Jack Inwood**

leading at the start. McLaren's Mini Cooper passed Marwood going into the hairpin, but Bruce had a tough time trying to catch the flying Grant. The two leaders circulated together until the last lap when McLaren took Grant on the right when Kerry anticipated Bruce going to the left as they entered the hairpin. Marwood won the 1301-2000 c.c. class, with Doc Langley (Humber 80) second, and Al McBeath won the over 2001 c.c. class in his 3.8 Jaguar.

Doc Langley defeated G. Lawrence (Peugoet) in the saloon handicap, Event 8, while McLaren chalked up another win in Event 11, a handicap race, ahead of G. Thomson's Zephyr, Marwood and Langley. In the final of the saloon scratch races, McBeath led the field at the start in his Jaguar while Grant and Marwood fought it out. McLaren took the Jaguar at the hairpin and the Mini Cooper went on to win. Grant was second in the up to 1300 c.c. class, with Marwood first in the 1301-2000 c.c. class, ahead of Langley. Finally, McBeath defeated McLaren by 0.1 of a second in the All Comers race after a close tussle, while Marwood was third and Langley fourth.

Jack Brabham also won the 8 lap final event, with Maggs second, Chris Amon third, and Angus Hyslop fourth. Barry Cottle won the sports car scratch race, with G. McRae (Maserarri) second in the up to 1500 c.c. class. J. Riley won the over 1501 c.c. class in his Monza Ferrari, while G. Richardson's Ferrari Berlinetta was second. Cottle also won the handicap sports race in his Lola, followed by D. Smyth (Buckler), J. Riley (Monza Ferrari) and A. Hurley (Cooper Bristol). C. Ngan in a Cooper won the 6 lap handicap race for sports cars ahead of A. Marshall (Buckler), W. Reid (T.R.3) and A. Hurley (Cooper Bristol). The inevitable Cottle won the sports car final of 10 laps with McRae second, while the big class was won by Richardson, with W. Reid second.

## Men & Machines

# Jack Brabham

***The first Australian to become world champion, he held the title in 1959, 1960 and 1966***

WHEN Jack Brabham lined up on the Long Beach starting grid on 27 March, at the wheel of a green-with-white-stripes "droop-snoot" 1958 Cooper-Climax (courtesy Tom Wheatcroft and his Grand Prix Collection), it was just as though the clock had been turned back 18 years and "Black Jack" had yet to win the first of his three World Championships.

Jack was six days short of his 50th birthday, well over five years into his retirement from motor racing, yet looking not one inch out of place in the environment of a single-seater cockpit. One had the impression that he would have been equally at home the following afternoon sitting in something much squatter, more powerful and wider-tyred, having a real go in the United States Grand Prix West rather than in the "demonstration" race for former champions which preceded it.

He is one of those fortunate people who never seems to age (you have to look pretty hard to spot those few grey hairs just above his ears) and who has the knack of slipping so comfortably into whatever he is doing that he seems to have been born to it. It was the case with his motor racing, and with his private flying; today it is the same way with his aircraft and marine activities in his native Sydney, or on his farm up-country – wearing the high-pressure business executive's suit in his penthouse one day, sweating it out at the wheel of his tractor the next . . . or donning his track suit for a spot of nostalgia and fun.

Throughout his racing career Jack Brabham was known as a driver of many skills but few words. He was a great listener and a deep thinker . . . but he tended to keep his thoughts to himself. Statistically, his three World Championships place him second equal to the great Juan Manuel Fangio (also at Long Beach that day) in the record book (the Argentinian took five titles). But a fairer assessment of him, perhaps, is to record that he was probably the most complete racing driver of them all, that is if you confine the task of the racing driver to that of winning races, rather than indulging in the trappings of stardom which these days racing successes tend to create.

There are some drivers who are natural race winners. There are others who can combine the competitive skill with an ability to race-tune their cars to peak performance. Jack Brabham went one stage further; he could climb out, roll up his sleeves and do the job himself. He surrounded himself with high-quality technical talent, from Ron Tauranac, his chief designer to his most junior mechanic, but if the need arose he could do any of their jobs himself – and frequently he did so. Many a late night was spent by the World Champion alone in his workshop, turning a new component on a lathe, achieving the standard of near-perfection which he demanded for the minutest detail of his cars.

It is no secret that it was Brabham's skill in the workshop as much as in the cockpit which enabled the Cooper Car Company to apply the mid-engine theme so successfully to Formula One in the late-fifties and emerge as double World Champions (Jack took the title in 1959 and 1960). It is also well-known that frustration at not being able to design and build the cars his own way contributed significantly to his decision to become a racing car manufacturer in his own right in 1961. It took him until 1966 to fulfil his ambition to become the first person to win a Grand Prix, in a car bearing his own name; he did it in the French Grand Prix, at Reims, in the Repco-engined Brabham, and began a formidable run of successes which were to lead to his third world title that year, to be followed by Denny Hulme's championship success in the second works car the following year. 1966 also brought Jack Brabham's most satisfying race victory of all – winning the German Grand Prix from Surtees and Rindt in atrociously wet and dangerous conditions.

It was in 1966, too, that Jack Brabham emerged as something of a humorist, to the amazement of all around him. He had had his 40th birthday on 2 April, and thereafter was bombarded with "Too old at 40," remarks, both in the Press and in the paddock. Three months of this was about all he was prepared to stand, so at Zandvoort he sent his wife Betty shopping for a "bolt-on" beard. Then, a few minutes before the start of the Dutch Grand Prix he disappeared into his pit, slipped on the beard, grabbed a jack handle for a walking stick, and "hobbled" down to the dummy grid on the arm of a Dutch race official; at the one-minute signal, he took off the beard . . . and went on to win the race!

Those of us who followed his 15 years in Europe at close quarters will retain several vivid memories of Jack Brabham. There was his extravagant tail-out technique of the 'fifties which left no doubt that he was a product of Australia's dirt tracks; later, that characteristic chin-in crouch in the cockpit when the pressure was on and he was really having a go; the remarkable sight of him climbing out after a particularly tough Grand Prix in roasting temperature without a trace of perspiration on his face; that black look of disgust when he lost his hard-won 1970 British Grand Prix through running out of fuel on the last lap; those electrifying Brabham starts (t'was said the starter would drop the flag as soon as he saw Jack's rear tyres begin to smoke!); and that day on the rostrum at Brands Hatch, in November 1970, when the grandstand stood to wish Jack and Betty *Bon Voyage* before they went back home. This year, their eldest son, Geoffrey, has come back to Europe, to drive one of Ron Tauranac's Ralts. If he stays to make half the motor racing history recorded by "The Old Man", he'll have done well. ●

*Jack Brabham, in his pre-Repco Brabham days, at the wheel of a Cooper.*

# JACK BRABHAM

## WORLD CHAMPION

### In the movies, the hero always wins the Championship in the car he built himself, but it's never happened in real life—till now.

Jack Brabham won the World Drivers Championship this year. He's done that before, in 1959 and 1960. He did it on a tight budget, which isn't exactly new. He also won the World Constructors Championship, which Enzo Ferrari, Colin Chapman, John Cooper, the BRM and Mercedes-Benz organizations, and others have done before. But no one has ever become World Champion in a car he built himself. Jack Brabham did it, and he's fair popping with quiet pride.

Who can blame him? When movie mogul John Frankenheimer was signing up teams for his forthcoming film, "Grand Prix," he thought so little of Brabham's seemingly outclassed car that Brabham's outfit was the only one of the bunch not on M-G-M's payroll.

Brabham took the pair of Championships in his 3-liter Brabham-Repco on less money than it cost his competitors to field losers. Brabham's effort wasn't quite on a shoestring, but now that it's all over, he's realized that with more money he might have fared worse.

What turned the trick for the darkly handsome Australian was an economy of man and machine. Simplicate and add lightness, as the English say. Brabham's engine, barely a souped-up little Oldsmobile V-8, was almost shamefully modest in its lack of pretentiousness. And in an era when practically every successful racing car is the latest, most sophisticated monocoque design, Brabham's winning chassis was an old space-frame model left over from the 1.5-liter formula.

If cost had been no object, Brabham & Co. might have succumbed to the temptation to multiply cylinders and camshafts and valves. The resulting engine might have been more powerful, but complication adds weight, lengthens development time and endangers reliability. Brabham didn't want potential horsepower, he wanted power *now,* while everyone else was still trying to sort out their engines on the test bench.

And Brabham didn't want too much power, only enough to get the job done. More power than the simple, single overhead camshaft Repco engine could produce might have been more than the car could handle . . . and, as time proved, more power wasn't necessary. "Four-hundred horsepower would have been an embarrassment to us this year," says New Zealander Phil Kerr, Brabham's manager.

Well, they were 100 horsepower short of this embarrassment, but quite unembarrassed by their engine's abundant torque. Nobody could have too much of that.

But car quality and driver ability are indispensable complements. One without the other draws no water. Viewed in this light, Brabham's chances didn't look too brilliant at the season's outset. Dan Gurney, who had won the only Championship races in a Brabham (in the pre-Repco days), wasn't available any more. His replacement, New Zealander Denis Hulme, although highly successful in lesser leagues, had yet to score in Formula One. Jack himself? Hmmm. *Maybe,* but he hadn't won a title race in six years. In the winter of 1960 he'd said he would retire from racing in "about two years' time." And, forgetting that Fangio was 47 when *he* pulled out, the barstool sages were resigning Brabham to a monoposto rocking chair. Hell, the man was *forty!*

So what? This isn't weightlifting or high jumping. Sheer muscle power doesn't win motor races. Jack himself says he never felt better in his life than he has this year, and probably feels (though characteristically he doesn't say), that he's never driven better. He's really in his professional prime these days.

If you're looking for one outstanding example of his superlative form at 40, the German GP supplies it. Holding off John Surtees (Ferrari) from the start of the second lap to the end of the fifteenth and last, over roads that were rain-drenched for most of the race and further lubricated by a greasy mixture of oil and rubber, Brabham made no mistakes. This performance, perhaps unparalleled at the Nürburgring under comparable conditions, underscores Phil Kerr's comment that Jack is "totally unflappable."

Australians don't seem to be subject to the English inhibition that prevents a man from declaring his ambitions for fear somebody will translate them as a boast that he's damn well going to *achieve* them. So Jack, if he's asked, makes no secret of his ardent hope to beat—or at least equal—Fangio's record of five World Championships. And

## To romantics who expect all GP drivers to be hell-raising hedonists, the sobersided Brabham must be a bit of a disappointment

why not, if the ball continues to lie right for him? He's won three already, and by the Fangio age scale, he still has seven years to win another three.

Brabham's phenomenal vitality and ox-like constitution are bywords among those close to him. "He's never beaten by anything," says Kerr. "He'll set himself schedules and objectives that you and I would consider ridiculous, impossible." Typically, his working day starts at 9:00 A.M. and finishes around 3:00 A.M. After a four-hour night—one in a long series, likely—he'll show up the next morning looking perfectly fresh and rested, in his characteristically equable frame of mind. When small-hours oil is being burnt in the racing workshops, it's tacitly understood that the mechanics won't go home until he does, and *he* won't while they're still at work, so a sort of insomniac cycle develops. The Brabham employees are a loyal bunch. Staff troubles of any kind are a rarity, and rarest of all among the Australasian element (all but two of the racing department's ten members are either Australians or New Zealanders). It's Brabham's personal example, not orders and exhortations, that has bred the prevalent anything-you-can-do spirit.

Brabham spends an average of seven months a year away from his adopted Britain, covers about 150,000 miles by air and land. Nearly half this distance is traveled in his own Beechcraft Queenair, self-piloted. In the space of three weeks during August of this year he flew from the Nürburgring to England, England to the United States, the U.S. to Australia, Australia back to England via the East, England to Sweden and Finland, thence to Denmark, England again, Finland again, and finally England. In the course of this hither and yonning, he raced at seven circuits, and also found time to talk business with Repco (Replacement Parts Co., a giant Australian operation) in Melbourne.

Brabham's renowned equability is not all-embracing. Two things in particular rile him. One, inefficiency and foot-dragging on the part of outside firms and individuals; and two, distortions of the Brabham story in the popular press. To read some British newspapers, you'd picture Brabham as a solitary blacksmith in a rawhide apron, shaping cars from the living metal on an anvil. Alone-he-dunnit is the recurrent theme, and a good story mustn't be spoiled by mentioning Jack's indispensable collaborators and aides. It should go without saying here that he never could have gotten off the ground without them.

High up on the but-for-whom list are Ron Tauranac, Jack's chief designer, and Roy Billington—Australian and New Zealander respectively. Tauranac and Brabham are almost ideally complementary, the former a highly qualified designer-draftsman with real mastery of the theory as well as the practice of chassis and suspension problems. What Jack lacks in engineering theory, his instinct, intuition, common sense and driving experience supply. The ideas he contributes are mostly workable, to say the least, but if they do have a flaw, Tauranac's background enables him to spot it immediately.

To romantics who expect all GP drivers to be hell-raising hedonists, pulsating with *brio* and *panache* and all that, the sobersided Brabham must be a bit of a disappointment: contentedly married, devoted father of three, minimal drinker (wine only), non-smoker, abstainer from riotous living in all its forms. On the other hand, he's a fully homologated nice-guy, famed for his absolute integrity. This unquestioned trustworthiness is largely responsible for the great success of his production racing cars (the world's best sellers) and for the support he's attracted from Repco and Honda. (Incidentally, he didn't solicit Formula Two engines from Honda—they were proffered. This deal has made him the envy of the entire F-2 world, since the Brabham-Hondas have yet to be beaten.)

Turning to Formula One, the 3-liter Brabham-Repco engine stands alone in being the only modern GP engine built around a stock block (the aluminum V-8 used in the early Oldsmobile F-85s). No 3-liter version was envisioned when the original project was launched early in 1964. The intention then was to build a 2.5-liter edition for Tasman events and a 4.3-liter sports/racing engine. The former was built and tested but not raced, and at this juncture or thereabouts,

Jack did a double take and proposed a 3-liter variant (85 x 55mm bore and stroke) for Formula One. The idea of using the F-85 block as a starting point had been his in the first place, by the way. The extensive design job involved was shared by Phil Irving, an Australian with history-making motorcycle engines to his credit, Frank Hallam of Repco, and Jack himself.

Irving, a freelance engineering consultant whom Repco had hired for this project, made the major contribution. *C/D* has already described the engine (*Technotes*, March 1966), but it's worth recalling that its numerous claims to the adjective "unique" include a non-hemispherical head—something that almost outranges living memory in the F-1 field. By now (post-Watkins Glen), the last vestige of kinship with the Olds engine has disappeared, and Repco blocks have replaced the F-85 castings.

The burning question now, of course, is what kind of engine will Brabham-Repco use in 1967 and thereafter? In the British technical press there have been kiteflying references to something with twelve cylinders, but Jack denies the existence of any such plans. One magazine quoted him as saying, "I think we'll need more cylinders by then," meaning next year. When queried on this, Brabham replied, "We may *need* more cylinders but I never said we'd *have* them, did I?" Nor, apparently will there be more camshafts and valves. The Brabham approach has traditionally been to find the right hardware first, then develop it further—not go off on a new tack with unproved equipment.

Brabham's relations with the press are conditioned by the conviction that if you don't have any particular tale to unfold, you might as well keep it folded. He's unfailingly friendly when you do meet him, but Jim Hall couldn't be more elusive if it's a question of sit-down talking sessions. He has firmly declined many offers from public relations bureaus to act as his mouthpiece, believing that deeds, not words, are the mainspring of effective publicity. True to his Honest-John scruples, he also refuses to endorse any product unless he's actually used it and shares the manufacturer's good opinion of it.

When the Repco sponsorship of Brabham was originally discussed, the principals drew up a list of five essentials for first-season success under the new formula that went like this: 1. Reliability, 2. Simplicity, 3. Lightness, 4. A driver of winning capability, 5. Horsepower—or at least an abundance of torque.

No rival, they figured, would be likely to meet four out of five of these requirements, whereas, with luck, they might. They further encouraged themselves with the thought that, except at Rheims and Monza, the championship races would be won and lost at three places—going into corners, going around corners, and coming out of corners. It was foreseeable that the Brabham-Repco would be light, thus giving its brakes less to do and taking care of the into-corners factor. Its lightness would help *in* corners, and more still during the post-corner acceleration phase. As for Rheims and Monza—where brute horsepower is all-important—it was reckoned that they could afford to lose both these rounds if performance came up to expectation on the remaining circuits. As it developed, they were premature in writing off Rheims; Jack not only won it, but he did so at an all-time record speed for a *grande epreuve*—136.7 mph.

In the light of wet-ink history, it's obvious that all five of the Brabham-Repco goals were achieved. The car, being simple, is light. It's reliable, largely for the same reason. Consistently in superb form, Jack certainly hasn't been driving like a man on the threshold of senility. With about 300 horsepower on call, the engine has been giving away less than the expected hundred horses to its stiffest competition. Moreover, it has a usable rev range of no less than 3500 rpm (4500 to 8000). One very cogent benefit of the Brabham-Repco's lightness is its exceptionally low fuel consumption. Tank capacity doesn't need to be any more than 35 gallons—about 20 gallons less than, for instance, the Cooper-Maseratis, and equal to a saving of some 140 lbs. in fuel alone. On the starting grid, with Jack aboard, the Brabham-Repco weighs as little as 1415 lbs., undercutting the Cooper by about 280 lbs.

Basically, Brabham blew off all comers this year because he had foresight. He knew that a simple, workable proposition would win him more Championship points than any temperamental combination, no matter how full of potential. Some critics originally charged Brabham with setting his sights too low . . . but that's where the target was. Next year, the target will move up, but Jack Brabham has probably drawn a bead on it already.

At speed on the circuit the Repco Brabham-DAF looks like any other racing car.

This is the original rear end layout of the car. Recent modifications have moved the heaviest mechanisms inboard.

WITH my hand on my heart, I can report that I have driven a Formula 3 car round a 30 mph corner on a rain-sodden race circuit with 8000 rpm showing on the clock, and still managed to survive. In fact, I never had a moment's anxiety.

In case you think this is a tall story concocted to get a works drive in a Formula 1 team, let me hasten to add that all the credit should go to Wim Hendriks, the brilliant Dutch engineer who designed and developed the Variomatic transmission for the little DAF road cars, and has now successfully applied the system to F3 single-seaters.

The story really goes back to 1964, when Hendriks was told he could experiment with a Variomatic automatic transmission unit in an Alexis chassis. The idea was to publicise the reliability and efficiency of the system, and to wipe out any doubts in the minds of would-be DAF customers as to the practicality of belt drive.

The Variomatic Alexis was given its first outing by Rob Slotemaker, who finished seventh overall in the F3 race preceding the Monaco Grand Prix in 1965, and was then handed over to Jack Brabham to test. Though somewhat shattered by the car's reluctance to go where he pointed it, Jack was sufficiently impressed with the transmission to agree to modify an existing F3 Repco Brabham chassis to accommodate it.

Since then, two more chassis have been built, 2½ inches longer than standard in wheelbase, and with the Cosworth-Ford engine moved 4 inches further forward. Some heartening results were achieved last season in conjunc-

A mechanic makes last-minute adjustments before Jack Brabham goes out for a test run.

tion with the Chequered Flag team, which entered the DAF-transmission car, and with Mike Beckwith, who did most of the driving.

The high spot of the season was at Zolder, in September, when in top F3 company Beckwith finished first in one race and third in two more, and DAF is now convinced that it has something worthwhile to offer racing, apart from any publicity rub-off which participation in it may give the company. For 1967, a two-car team is being operated for DAF by the Chequered Flag, with Mike Beckwith and a promising young Dutchman, Gijs van Lennep, as regular drivers.

Track-testing the Repco Brabham-DAF meant a break from the Brands Hatch tradition, and a trip over to Zolder (just on the Belgian side of the border with Holland, and conveniently close to the DAF headquarters at Eindhoven). Roughly 2½ miles round, it has something of the flavor of both the Nurburgring and Zandvoort, with a potential lap time of 1 mile 41 seconds for a Formula 3 car in the dry.

Unfortunately, the first spots of rain fell just before I climbed into the cockpit, and the track became wetter and wetter as the day progressed until even van Lennep was barely hitting the 2-minute barrier. Fortunately, that was the only thing we hit all day, although the four of us who drove the car amassed a fair number of spins between us!

For anyone familiar with the Variomatic system provided on DAF passenger cars, the gearing provided by the twin belts running in variable-diameter pulleys is influenced by a system of bobweights acting on the primary pulleys, with a supplementary variation in ratio being achieved by manifold pressure or vacuum operating on a diaphragm adjacent to the pulleys.

The transmission requirements on the race track, of course, are very different from those on the road, mainly because in racing (and in particular when racing with small-capacity, high-revving engines) you use only a small percentage of the available rev range, and cannot afford any time lag while the revs climb up to an effective level after a period of over-run.

The manifold-influenced diaphragm, therefore, has been replaced by an ingenious device which ensures that the gearing is automatically lowered immediately the engine goes on to overrun, and in this way the revs are kept to a minimum of around 7500 rpm, even when coming into the slowest corner.

The device consists of a peg which engages in a spiral groove cut out of the wall of a cylindrical cage mounted on the axis of the front pulleys. The peg itself, mounted outboard of the left-hand pulley, is driven by the hollow countershaft, but the cage merely floats on the outside of the countershaft, and is coupled to a thin rod running inside the shaft which, in turn, is connected to the outside surface of the pulley on the other side of the car.

With the engine driving the car at maximum speed, the peg is hard up against one end of the groove, while the cage has floated away from the adjacent pulley, and by means of the thin rod has also pulled the faces of the offside pulley together to give the highest possible gearing. But immediately the engine backs off, the countershaft will have the effect of braking the peg's motion while the cylindrical cage continues to revolve at its former speed.

**ABOVE LEFT: The original rear end layout of the Repco Brabham-DAF. ABOVE: This is how the latest model looks with its driving pulleys swapped about.**

# *It's automatic ...AND FAST*

This causes the peg to move along the spiral groove, the cage to move inwards, the pulley faces to part, and the gearing to drop.

A centrifugal clutch, encased in a steel-lined aluminium housing, transmits the drive from the crankshaft to the bevel gears on the primary countershaft by means of three spring-controlled shoes, the spring tension being sufficient to delay engagement until approximately 5500 rpm (instead of around 1000 rpm on the DAF 44). The springs are supported by dowels to prevent them breaking loose at high speed.

On an earlier installation, the primary countershaft was placed behind the secondary shaft, resulting in a rather tailheavy chassis, while overall gearing was adjusted by means of drop gears on the output shaft.

On the latest and most successful application, however, the primary shaft is ahead of and the secondary shaft immediately behind the final-drive line, and a train of three gears runs forward from the secondary shaft to the differential to establish the overall gearing. The primary shaft gear reduction is 2.54 to 1, and with a 3.25 to 1 differential (3.46 and 3.70 diffs. are also available), overall gearing can be varied between 5.33 and 17.20 to 1. Weight distribution, with driver, is 45/55 with the latest set-up.

Climbing aboard, the first unusual feature you see is the matching pair of rev counters. One, in fact, acts as a speedometer (after appropriate conversion), and is used to establish overall gearing requirements on new circuits. It is not used during racing, and had been disconnected before the test. The conventional gear shift has been replaced by a simple right-handed push-pull lever, giving neutral or drive, with a spring-loaded flap beneath guarding a further movement backwards to get reverse.

Lifting the front body sections reveals a two-in-one brake pedal, the conventional clutch pedal having been coupled to the brake to offer either right or left-foot braking. By the time I had slipped right down in the cockpit I found that my right leg was bent too much to get to the brake pedal comfortably, and so I used my left leg and the left pedal throughout the test. Gijs van Lennep, incidentally, is convinced that right-foot braking is the answer for both speed and accuracy.

Wet-track starts are usually tricky, but with Variomatic there is no drama at all. It virtually eleminates wheelspin on the most slippery of surfaces and you can floor the accelerator and accelerate smoothly ahead while all the boys with conventional transmissions are anxiously watching their rev counters and correcting their slides. For a racing start the technique seems to be to hold the engine at around 5000 rpm until a second or two before flag-fall, then build it up to 6000 to 6500 rpm, holding the car back on the footbrake, then simultaneously lift one foot and drop the other as the flag comes down.

The first few laps were spent in finding out where the corners went. The wide pit straight narrows down into a tight 90-degree left-hander, followed by a short straight leading into a double-right-hander needing two distinct stabs and adding up to about 180 degrees (very weird, that one!). Another short straight alongside a canal leads into a third right-hander and on to the main straight, parallel to and behind the pits. A fast left-hand curve leads uphill beneath a pedestrian bridge and over a sharp blind hump where the car feels as though it gets airborne but doesn't quite.

In the dry the 'stars' take this flat-out in top, building up speed down the other side and through the left-hander at the foot of the incline before braking for a slowish right-hander. Almost immediately after comes another right-hander, then a left curve followed by a drop down to the right-handed hairpin (and a gate barring the escape road!). The up-hill run back to the pits straight is punctuated by two left-handed 'S' bends, the first of which can be straight-lined, and the second taken just about flat, I should think, in the dry.

The first lap or two seemed very strange, and I never realised quite to what extent you rely upon your ears when driving. The most difficult thing is to judge your approach speed into corners with the engine revving away behind you, and inevitably you err on the slow side. It takes time, but you have to almost completely disregard what you hear and try to concentrate on the car's feel as you sort out breaking points.

The size of the bobweights had been adjusted on this car to allow a peak crankshaft speed of 9200 rpm, but 9000 rpm comes up very soon after leaving a corner with the power full on. It took the length of the back straight to collect those last 200 revs, and as you wait for the speed to rise with a background noise of an almost constant engine note the power limitations imposed by Formula 3 regulations are brought into very clear focus. I hasten to add that, as lap times have proved, the DAF-transmission car accelerates just as quickly (or slowly!) as an equivalent F3 car with a four-speed gearbox.

# THE WORLD ACCORDING TO JACK

***HE WON THE FIRST OF HIS THREE TITLES 40 YEARS AGO AND THE LAST, UNIQUELY, WAS IN A CAR BEARING HIS OWN NAME. AND, AS HE TELLS ADAM COOPER, WHAT STILL MATTERS MOST TO SIR JACK BRABHAM IS RACING.***

FORTY YEARS AFTER HE WON HIS FIRST WORLD CHAMPIONSHIP, Sir Jack Brabham is showing no signs of slowing down. He is always in demand for historic events and PR appearances, and he never turns down the chance to get back behind the wheel. As he showed at the Goodwood Revival Meeting last September, just pootling round in a museum piece is not the Brabham style; he still likes to hang the tail out. The spirit still burns and man, now 73, still drives. Hard.

"I really enjoy getting back into those old cars," he smiles. "It feels just like old times, gives me a little bit of a spurt and stops me from getting old!" When will he finally give it up?

"I'm going to have a think about it when I'm 75, and if I still want to do it I'll review it again when I'm 80. When I get in a motor car I don't feel any different."

Sir Jack Brabham is our oldest living Formula One World Champion. A handful of other F1 drivers bridged the enormous gulf from the 1950s to the 1970s (Jo Bonnier, Graham Hill, Bruce McLaren and Dan Gurney), but none started quite as early as Brabham, who made his GP debut at Aintree in 1955. Only Jack raced against the Mercedes W196 and the Lotus 72. During a remarkable career he won three titles, the last with his own team and car. And he was still winning when he reluctantly walked away from the sport in 1970, at the age of 44.

**"I never used to worry too much about the press, but that was a mistake"**

And yet somehow his achievements have been taken for granted by the history books. Ask anyone to list the Top Ten of all time, and Brabham's name is never considered. Extend the query to the Top 20, and he might just crop up in the low teens, alongside drivers who didn't win a single title, never mind three. Stirling Moss and Jim Clark dominated the headlines when Jack was racing, and they still do.

"I think it's just that I didn't piss in the press's pockets as much as other people," he grins. "Being an Australian doesn't help over in this country. I never used to worry too much about what the press wrote about me, but, in retrospect, that probably was a mistake on my part."

Jack was never very dashing or glamorous. He was a man of few words, always characterised as a thinker, a dour technician who often won races through stealth. That sort of low-key style rarely captures the public imagination. But when the mood took him Brabham was also a hard racer who could fight with the best.

The World Championship was not on the unknown Australian's mind when he first came to Britain. Already pushing 30, he didn't seem to have much of a future, but within a few years he helped to turn Grand Prix racing upside down – or rather back to front.

"All I was interested in was just doing some motor racing. I never even thought about a World Championship or whatever. It took me a year to find out what motor racing was all about over here, and luckily I got in tow with John Cooper, and he gave me a job at the works putting cars together and things like that. Eventually I drove for him, and that was really how it all started.

"He let me build a car in the workshop, revolving around the little Bobtail sportscar. I put a 2-litre Bristol in it, and that really became Cooper's first F1 car. We had a little trouble with it up at Aintree, and the clutch fell out of it before the end of the race, but I then took it home and won the Australian GP in 1955."

A tremendous rapport developed between Brabham and Cooper, the underdogs who took on the might of Italy, and cheekily outflanked Vanwall and BRM to become Britain's premier racing team.

"It wasn't long before we realised that there was a lot of potential at Cooper's, but even then we didn't think that we would win a World Championship so quickly. The rear-engined car was obviously the way to go, and luckily Coventry-Climax built a 2.5-litre engine for us, which really put us in the driving seat. We went straight out and won the Championship in '59 and '60. Without that engine we wouldn't have been able to achieve it."

The double title was a tremendous achievement for the little manufacturer. Jack was far more than just the driver. He was at the heart of the team, spearheading development – especially the 1960 'lowline' model, in which he scored five straight victories.

"The most enjoyable win was Reims. We were told there's no way we were going to beat the Ferraris there. We managed to do it, and it was a great thrill. In all my years of racing I never got to drive a Ferrari, but I had a lot of pleasure beating them. It was a very interesting time for me, being so involved in it, being part of it. Going all round the continent with John was a lot of fun on its own, apart from the racing. It was a big advantage to me to have some mechanical knowledge, but there were times when I backed off in the car when I probably didn't need to, and lost races by doing that. At the same time at least I didn't drive it into the ground like some of the other drivers."

The spell was broken by the switch to 1.5-litre rules in 1961. After an unsuccessful final year with Cooper the only highlight came by shaking up the establishment at the Indianapolis 500. "It was very different. They called our Cooper the funny car, because it was so different to what they had. Then they said it shouldn't be painted green, because that was bad luck there. Then they caught me eating peanuts, and they said you shouldn't eat peanuts in the pits, that's unlucky. The other thing they said was you mustn't bring a woman into the pits. I couldn't find one so I couldn't do that."

A difficult 1961 helped Jack made the bold decision to build his own car. Again, he was breaking new ground; drivers had run their own teams before, but no established star had gone the whole hog as a manufacturer.

"I had a friend in Australia, Ron Tauranac, and I talked him into coming over. We started our own company in '62. It was a gamble, but I had a lot of confidence in Ron's ability. The two of us were a good combination. We were short of money and couldn't do it properly, and it took a few years really to get going. We were also starting to build production cars to be able to afford to go GP racing. That really took a bit of doing."

Did his driving actually suffer because of the outside pressures? "I don't know whether it affected it, but we certainly didn't do all that well for a while. We had the incentive to keep going with our own car, and we thought we'd get there eventually, which we did."

Jack didn't win a single World Championship race during the 1.5-litre era, although team-mate Dan Gurney gave the team its first successes. "It was good news when they brought in the 3-litre formula. It really made the cars worth driving, so that you could call it F1 again. There's no way you could call those 1500cc machines Formula One."

Having already been caught out by the slump at Cooper, Jack couldn't let his team be left in the lurch by a rule change. He did such a good job that his cars dominated the first two years of the new formula.

"It was a bit of foresight on my part. Our problem was we just didn't have access to a 3-litre engine we could put in a car and go racing with." History recalls the solution was a triumph called Repco. Jack won four races in 1966 to become the first and, to date, only man to take the title in his own car. But it was not without its troubles.

"Trying to work 12,000 miles away from your engine builder wasn't easy. We lost so many parts in air freight – we even lost a complete engine for three weeks. The thing had been outside a hangar in the rain before somebody found it."

The following year honours went to Denny Hulme, before the Repco was superseded by the DFV. In 1968, Jack earned a solitary fifth place. He joined the DFV hordes the next year, and while he didn't win, two pole positions reminded everyone that Black Jack had by no means lost interest.

By then he was under pressure to return to Australia to spend more time with sons Geoffrey, Gary and David. He planned his retirement for the end of the 1969 season when, at 43, he would already be one of the sports elder statesmen. As you can read in Alan Henry's accompanying story, the plan all went up in smoke when Rindt chose to stay put with Chapman rather than return to Brabham. Jack had no choice but to drive for one more year, and nearly enjoyed a remarkable swansong.

He won at Kyalami, took pole at Jarama, and outran Rindt around Monaco until an infamous last corner mishap saw him stuck in the fence as the Austrian swept by. He led again in the British GP before his season dissolved in a series of mechanical retirements; he had already scored the last points of his Formula One career. His final outing was at the Mexican GP on October 25, but engine problems forced him out. Was it hard to accept it was all over as he packed away his gear?

"I was stuck with it, I couldn't change it. It was a dreadful feeling really. I felt very sad, and I couldn't believe it had come to an end. I just had to grit my teeth, and say that's it. I had made my mind up and I'd got to get on with it." At least he had left knowing he was still quick enough to win. A talent such as his was not one to watch wither on the vine. Just as Jack was smart enough to know how to start in F1 and start his own F1 team, so he was also smart enough to know when to quit.

"I didn't feel I was giving up racing because I couldn't do the job. I felt just as competitive then as at any other time, and I really should have won the championship in 1970. I have no idea, but I think I could have gone on at least another three or four years. The press didn't help either – they kept calling me the old man of motor racing, at 44! In those days 44 was old, but today, particularly if you go to America, there are plenty of people racing well in their 50s."

Although he'd previously helped youngsters like Bruce McLaren, Hulme and Rindt, Jack chose not to stay on and run others. Again, there really was no decision to be made; owning the team would have kept him out of Australia as much as driving for one, so it had to go too.

"To me all my enjoyment I have had over the years was never just driving, but being involved in the cars and the building of the cars. I got just as much pleasure from that. But the family wanted me to go back to Australia, so I was stuck with that. If I'd stayed I would have been involved with the team, probably doing testing and all that sort of thing. It really wouldn't have been any different to driving.

**"I really should have won the championship in 1970 as well"**

"I'd have been a lot better off if I'd stayed. That was another mistake in my life, but sometimes family pressures don't allow you to make the decisions you'd like to. Ron took it all over and it wasn't long before he got fed up with it and sold it to Bernie Ecclestone."

Jack may look back now with regrets, but at least he got out of the sport in one piece. During his final Grand Prix season McLaren, Piers Courage and Rindt were killed, and the ensuing three or four years extracted a terrible toll. "It's very sad, actually. Every now and then I pick up an old programme and look at it. I saw one from Monaco '58 and more than half the drivers are not there any more. It's incredible how many friends we've lost over the years. I always remember winning the Belgian GP in 1960, when we had two drivers killed in separate accidents in one race."

Jack insists it wasn't just good fortune which ensured his survival over such a long career.

"I'm like everyone else, all drivers think that it's not going to happen to them, but one of the things that got me through it all was that I had very good control over my emotions and my abilities. I knew when to knock off, and I wasn't too proud to lift my foot if I felt that was what was needed. There were a lot of people out there who didn't lift their foot at the right time and are not here to talk about it today."

Jack had only three significant accidents in his entire career. In Portugal in 1959 he was sent flying by an errant backmarker. Later he was put off the road by tyre failures in testing at Silverstone and, in his final year, at Zandvoort.

"It rolled three or four times through a wire fence. When I came to rest I was upside down and I couldn't get out, as the wire was wrapped around the car. I was sitting there hanging in the seatbelts. Fuel was running out of the car, although luckily it was disappearing into the sand. Being a test day it took forever for somebody to come over..."

***Clockwise from top left: Brabham and McLaren, Cooper team-mates; Brabham alongside Clark (no 1) at Reims – "he was not in Moss's or Rindt's class"; more autographs in his final season at the 1970 South African GP with son David, later a racer himself; working hard to stave off Moss – "the one to beat. He never, ever had an off-day"***

Jack has a unique perspective on 15 years of technical progress.

"From 1955-70 we saw a lot of changes, and I felt part of it, because with the rear-engined Cooper we felt we gave everyone the message "if you don't put the engine in the back you're not going to catch us." Colin Chapman was one of them. He was pretty pig-headed about having the engine in the front, but he couldn't compete with us."

So which period did he most enjoy?

"The 3-litre cars from '66 onwards. It was our own car, and we did well with it. We won the constructors' title twice."

Jack has no doubts about the greatest driver he raced against.

"I raced Fangio a couple of times, but Moss was the one I had a lot of dices with and learned a lot from. He was the man to beat, and it was a great challenge for me. Moss never, ever had an off-day. He was a competitor from when the flag dropped to the end. Some of the others were good on some days but not every day, and things had to go right for them all the time. With Moss it didn't matter what he was driving. Probably the next best was Rindt."

And what of Clark? Jack's view will surprise.

"He was good too, but I don't think he was in the Moss or Rindt class from a speed point of view. They were two very fast drivers. It was the era when Clark had the best car. Lotus was on top, and Jimmy drove it well. But he would have his off days – he wasn't fantastic every time he sat in the car, like Moss.

"I suppose Jackie Stewart was the best of the next era. Since the 1970s Senna's obviously the best driver to come along. He was a very forceful driver. Stewart was a bit like me – we won, but we wouldn't stick our necks out to do it. Our own safety was more important. Schumacher makes the odd mistake, but when you look at the rest, he's the quickest and best driver today.

"Personally I don't think F1 would be as good to be in today as it was when we were driving. The driver role is not all that concerned with the car any more; you don't get involved in the technical side. As for driving, they go round on rails, they don't have to change gear – just press a few buttons and computers do the lot for them. I just don't think the challenge is as good."

Jack still attends GPs, although this year he missed his home race because of business commitments in England. His famous garages in Worcester Park (est 1961) and Ewell (1965) still take up a lot of his time. Through them he's retained links with a little corner of suburbia which holds a lot of memories, since both Cooper and his own team were once based nearby. He's almost certainly the only man to have driven an F1 car on the A3.

"It was about 10am on Sunday morning, and we'd just got the Cooper finished. We decided that we'd have to give it a run, just drive it round the block. But I ended up going up the Kingston bypass, down to the Hook roundabout and back again. When I got to Ewell I noticed a police car chasing me. I raced down to the garage, went in and shouted out to John to shut the door as I skidded to a halt. We went upstairs in time to watch the police looking in the window to see if they could see anybody. We had to try it out, didn't we?..."

***Clockwise from top left: with the Cooper team in France '61; Jack's debut in Cooper's first F1 car, the Bristol-engined Bobtail he built, at the British GP 1955; Brabham in discussion with Ron Tauranac, his design partner and later owner of the team; 43 and still flying - Jack at Barcelona in 1969, the year he wanted to retire, though circumstances forced him to drive in '70 too***

ESSO congratulate

# JACK BRABHAM

on the unique achievement of
building, entering and driving his own
Repco Brabham to become

# WORLD CHAMPION

for the third time since 1959
using Esso fuels and lubricants—of course!

**4**th **BELGIAN** Grand Prix
**1**st **FRENCH** Grand Prix
**1**st **BRITISH** Grand Prix
**1**st **DUTCH** Grand Prix
**1**st **GERMAN** Grand Prix

Esso

**PUT A TIGER IN YOUR TANK WITH ESSO EXTRA**

**Australian Grand Prix**

Right: Jack Brabham slowly whittles down John Surtees' lead.

Below: New Zealand driver, Jim Palmer, dressed according to the Warwick Farm fashion. Very dark goggles were worn to cut down the sun's glare and a scarf protected the face from flying stones.

Photographs — B. Polain.

# Jack wins in the old home town

THE official news release handed out after the 1963 Australian Grand Prix at Warwick Farm on February 10 said the weather was "Hot and Sunny". This may convey a lot of things to a lot of people but I doubt if many will get the message as to just what conditions were like when Jack Brabham won his second G.P. and his first race in Sydney since he left five years ago to make his fortune overseas.

It was hot as only Sydney can be hot at this time of the year. With the sun beating down steadily and without even a suspicion of a breeze to help cool things down the air above the track heated up to over 130 degrees. In the cockpit of some cars the temperature was a sizzling 180 degrees and down where the radiators were in the rear engined cars it was hot enough to severely scorch the soles of the drivers' shoes so that at the end of a race their feet looked like lobsters. In a front engined car things were even worse.

The conditions make Brabham's win even more meritorious. Not only was he the man with the best machinery (the Repco-Brabham-Climax of his own design), or the fastest driver over 45 laps, but also the toughest of them all.

A crowd of 40,000 turned out to see the race which featured a large field of internationals and Australia's leading drivers who, for the first time since Stan Jones cleaned up in the Maybach in New Zealand, had cars which were equal to anything the stars could bring in from overseas.

Scuderia Veloce chief, David Mckay, managed to get hold of the car which Brabham raced at the G.P. in Perth late last year and in New Zealand, Bib Stillwell had Brabham fly him out a brand new one from England and Brabham contented himself with another new car which almost didn't make it in time. The "Brabham" was loaded on a boat in England after a delay caused by the boat going to the aid of the P. and O liner Canberra which was stranded after a fire, the car could not be off loaded anywhere else but Melbourne as an even faster machine, Donald Campbell's Bluebird, was blocking the entrance to the hold.

When the car was finally off loaded Brabham had nowhere near enough time to prepare a car which had never been raced.

John Surtees arrived with a 2,700 c.c. Climax powered Lola entered by the Bowmaker Credit team who had also entered Tony Maggs in a similar car and New Zealand driver, J. Palmer, in a Cooper Climax.

Scuderia Veloce had a second string going with Chris Amon at the wheel of the ex-McLaren 2.5 litre Cooper Climax. Others who arrived with 2.5 litre cars were John Youl, Cooper; Tony Shelly (N.Z.), Lotus; and Graham Hill who had the revolutionary Ferguson with a 2.5 litre Climax motor.

Hill was undoubtedly the man everybody wanted to see in action but troubles in practice and in the race itself prevented him from demonstrating any world championship form. The Ferguson, although of great technical interest, was a "fizzer" as far as the race was concerned and was no match for the more orthodox cars.

While we appreciated the chance of seeing the Ferguson in action we would have liked to see a reserve car for Hill to climb into when the highly complicated machine indicated it was not going to give its best.

Four times G.P. winner, Lex Davison, raced his 2.7 litre Cooper and also brought the Lukey Muffler Ford Galaxie for Touring car events.

Three under 1500 c.c. cars competed in the G.P. for a special class prize. Leo Geoghegan had a Lotus 20b, Frank Matich had an Elfin and Bob Holden entered the Lynx Peugeot.

First official practice was held on the Saturday afternoon the day before the big race and John Surtees took no time at all to get down to a 1 min. 38.9 secs. lap. This was the fastest for the session and compared favourably with McLaren's lap record of 1 min. 37.5 seconds established last year.

The man who made everybody stop thinking of cold beer for a moment or two was Frank Matich. He fairly sizzled round the circuit in the little Ford-engined Elfin to beat his 1 min. 41.6 seconds class record with a time of 1 min. 40.4 seconds — third fastest time for a session which included some of the world's fastest cars and drivers!

In the second practice Surtees brought his time down to 1 min. 38.1 secs. to take pole position on the grid. Beside him was none other than David McKay who had found the new Brabham very much to his liking and had made second fastest practice time. Hopes rose as all and sundry discussed the chances of a local driver cleaning up the imports. Bruce McLaren took the third spot on the front row.

Frank Matich got his time down to 1 min. 40 secs. dead in the second practice but so did Chris Amon and Tony Maggs.

Hill was having trouble with the Ferguson's carburettor. He had either full power or no power at all and at one stage, when the car slid a fraction in a corner during practice, he put his foot down to find absolutely nothing and left the track in a tyre screeching spin. Still he finally got things right enough to get on the third row of the grid but when everybody else was packing up to go home mechanics were still working feverishly trying to find out why the carburettors would not carburete. Whatever it was they couldn't find it.

Brabham made the last row of the grid with a car that obviously needed plenty of adjustment before it could turn in a race-winning lap. But as Jack designed this car himself he knew exactly what would do what and working into the night and early the next morning he managed to get things more to his liking.

As we told you earlier race day was a scorcher. Before the race mechanics broke the hearts of all who had admired the sleek styling of the big cars by cutting gaps here and there to let a little air in to the drivers. Lex Davison had come prepared with a neat little vent into the front of the Cooper just in front of the windscreen but the other cars looked as though a maniac had been let loose with an axe.

Before the race itself holes were hammered in cans to provide makeshift showers if any driver was forced to pull into the pits and Jack Brabham filled his crash helmet with ice cubes and stuffed the lote on his head.

Precisely at 2 p.m. on raceday, drivers in the A.G.P. were driven around the circuit in a fleet of white M.G.-A's. Brabham alone failed to mak ean appearance, he was still busy working on replacing fuel lines and final last minute preparation. The night before, new engine mounts had been fitted to the car.

On their return, drivers took out their racing machinery for a slow warm-up lap after which beach umbrellas and tarpaulins were used to cover up the cockpits.

Grid positions were as follows:—

| | | |
|---|---|---|
| D. McKAY<br>(Repco B'ham Clim.)<br>1 m. 38.9 s. | B. McLAREN<br>(Cooper Climax)<br>1 m. 38.8 s. | J. SURTEES<br>(Lola Climax)<br>1 m. 38.1 s. |
| C. AMON<br>(Cooper Climax)<br>1 m. 40 s. | A. MAGGS<br>(Lola Climax)<br>1 m. 40 s. | |
| G. HILL<br>(Ferguson Climax)<br>1 m. 40.6 s. | L. DAVISON<br>(Cooper Climax)<br>1 m. 40.3 s. | F. MATICH<br>(Elfin Ford)<br>1 m. 40 s. |
| L. GEOGHEGAN<br>(Lotus 20B)<br>1 m. 41.1 s. | J. YOUL<br>(Cooper Climax)<br>1 m. 40.9 s. | |
| J. PALMER<br>(Cooper Climax)<br>1 m. 42.3 s. | T. SHELLY<br>(Lotus Climax)<br>1 m. 41.7 s. | B. STILLWELL<br>(Repco B'ham Clim.)<br>1 m. 41.4 s. |
| F. GARDNER<br>(Cooper Maserati)<br>1 m. 47.3 s. | R. HOLDEN<br>(Lynx Peugeot)<br>1 m. 46.1 s. | J. BRABHAM<br>(Repco B'ham Clim.)<br>1 m. 44.4 s. |

The resplendently dressed starter, Stirling Moss, sent the field away in a tight bunch with only Frank Gardner left on the line. Surtees was well away, with McKay close when the Cooper Maserati's transmission finally called it a day. Behind and apparently unworried by the fact that McLaren was breathing down his neck. Graham Hill showed the Ferguson's four-wheeled drive to advantage as he moved up several places on initial acceleration off the line.

End of lap one saw race order: Surtees, McKay, McLaren, Hill, Maggs and Amon. McLaren moved up one placing but lost this advantage when he spun on the second lap at Creek Corner — a tight hairpin at the end of Hume Straight. Lap times were slower than expected as the circuit was very slippery. No doubt the hot weather contributed towards this, plus the fact that there had been four races preceeding the main event. Adding to the problem was oil escaping from John Youl's Cooper which was circulating in tenth position. Youl's problem was a loose sump plug and he subsequently retired at half distance through lack of oil.

McLaren's spin had cost him a number of places and he rejoined the race in ninth position. Meanwhile Brabham who was sixth on lap two moved to fourth on lap three and on the following round settled for some comfortable motoring in third spot. On the fourth lap Surtees had a five seconds lead over McKay, followed by Brabham, Maggs, Hill, Stillwell, Davison, McLaren, Amon, Youl, Shelly, Palmer, Matich, Geoghegan and Holden.

Brabham's car seemed to be performing well with just a puff of blackish/blue smoke coming from the exhaust on the overrun and also as the throttle opened. After several laps behind McKay, during which time Surtees had increased his lead, Brabham made a forward move and closed right up on the leading "local" driver. He tailed McKay through Polo and slipped into second place on the short straight to Ledger. This left Surtees wtih a nine seconds lead which he improved to over thirteen seconds, whilst Brabham remained in second place.

Jim Palmer retired with a broken steering arm on his Cooper and after his twelfth lap Lex Davison pulled into the pits for a new wheel. Davison had cracked a wheel after scraping a fence in the esses and was to lost 10 laps fitting a new one. The following lap saw Surtees lap Bob Holden and two circuits later Matich passed Shelly on brakes into the Causeway. Graha mHill had been following Stillwell for many laps when he too decided it was time to pass. Using the excellent accelera-tion out of slow corners that the Ferguson is noted for, he strongly challenged Stillwell on the run to Polo corner. Despite such a strong challenge from the world champion himself, Stillwell resisted the attempt to shoulder him out of the way and held his own. Having made the attempt to pass, Hill then dropped back, being slowly baked in the tremendous heat which flowed in the cockpit from the engine, and remained behind the blue Brabham for the remainder of the race.

Leaving the Causeway on his 20th lap Surtees spun com-pletely around twice without leaving the track. Still with his engine running the car came to rest pointing in the right direc-tion with the rear wheels just touching the dirt on the inside of the circuit. This error, after 35 minutes or so of dicing on a greasy track must have been a great disappointment to Surtees as he rejoined the race with now only a six seconds advantage over Brabham.

Brabham's pit passed on the good news and he began lapping in the "late" 1 min. 41 secs. to whittle down Surtees lead by up to two seconds per lap. Davison was now back in the race and was leading McLaren and McKay — McLaren had moved by McKay just three laps previous. As the leaders, Surtees and Brabham, completed their 25th lap, Davison spun at the entrance to the Causeway. McKay took advantage of this and cheekily slipped past McLaren to move back into third spot but kept this placing for one lap only before McLaren returned permanently to this position.

Interest centred on the leaders as Brabham caught Surtees on lap 29 and followed him closely for two more laps. Streak-ing down Hume Straight at some 140 m.p.h. the blue Brabham with the goid nose pulled out and passed the Lola as the two cars were braked for the slow hairpin corner. There was no need to look — the roar of the crowd told of "J.B." taking the lead.

From there on it was Brabham's race as Surtees did not attempt to regain the lead. By this time Surtees was suffering from the heat — as was everybody — and evidently decided to finish in a sure second place rather than risk everything in chal-lenging a man so determined to win in front of his "old home town".

After his victory lap Jack Brabham pulled up at the finish line before hordes of excited photographers and officials. Later Brabham mentioned that this win was one of the most satis-fying experiences of his career!!

The prize presentation was executed by Stirling Moss, who expertly brought to light various highlights of the race, together with the fact that Surtees had set fastest lap although Brabham had equalled it later in the event. This time of 1 min. 40.2 secs. (80.84 m.p.h.) indicated the hazardous nature of the track compared with McLaren's fastest lap in 1962 of 1 min. 37.5 secs. Brabham's time for the 101 miles round the 2¼ mile circuit was 1 hr. 16 min. 34.1 secs. — an average of 79.57 m.p.h. After receiving of his prize, Brabham in turn presented McKay with a canteen of cutlery for being the first Australian licence-holder to finish the race.

A number of smaller events made up the full programme. The first was for selected production sports cars over five laps. This event provided a close finish when Fletcher (A/H 100S) pulled out and passed Lawler (Daimler SP250) in the final run to the checkered flag.

Racing cars over a similar distance saw Bryan Thompson (Cooper Climax S/C) lead throughout followed by Geoghegan and Ferguson. Kelley (Cooper) followed after a good run through the field from the back row of the grid. Also Collerson (Jolus) improved his position after an overheated clutch slowed his run over the opening laps.

The big boys trundled out their sports cars for a ten lapper but the interest lagged after Matich (Lotus 19) slipped by Stillwell (Cooper Monaco) under brakes into Polo on the second lap. The second lap also saw Greg Cusack leave the circuit at the Western crossing as he was in hot pursuit of Ian Geoghegan in a Lotus 23. Cusack's Lola struck an embank-ment and landed on its nose but luckily without rolling on the driver.

Touring cars in two classes to 1600 c.c. provided one of the best events of the day. George Reynolds in his VW won the larger capacity division but came home in third place outright behind the smaller "Mini bricks" driven by Peter Manton and Ron Hodgson. Hodgson pushed Manton all the way but was unable to pass despite establishing a new class lap record of 2 min. 2.8 secs.

Bob Jane ran away with the G.T. event and the crowd con-centrated on the dice between Lindsay (Holden) and Richard-son (Ferrari Berlinetta). Much to the spectators' enjoyment, Holden triumphed over Ferrari.

Ten laps for a competitive showing of F.J. entries promised interest as Leo Geoghegan took up pole position in his Lotus 22. Geoghegan had put the fastest practice lap at a staggering 1 min. 40.9 secs. and shared the front row with Gardner (Brabham) and Cusack (Elfin). Geoghegan led from the start followed by Gardner with Cusack moving into third spot ahead of Scott (Lotus) in the second lap. Cusack's move looked dicy as he went under Scott on the righthander into the rough Northern crossing. In the closing stages Gardner — a driver with a big reputation overseas — pushed Geoghegan harder and harder trying to find an opening, almost managing to get by under him at Polo on the eighth lap. Seconds after, Nolan spun on this corner to lose two places. The following lap Gardner nearly made it again and on the final lap they were side by side from Polo to Ledger. Nevertheless at the finish it was the Lotus leading by a mere two tenths of a second. Geoghegan pulled off the circuit at Paddock Bend and was lifted exhausted from the car at the rear entrance to the pits.

Finally the programme drew to a close with the staging of the over 1600 c.c. touring car event which Bob Jane won con-vincingly from Lex Davison driving Len Lukey's Ford Galaxie. Although Davison lost time when he spun at the Causeway on the fourth lap, the Jaguar seemed in command at the time. Despite the greasy track Bruce McPhee lowered his own class record to 2 min. 2 secs. — a remarkable achievement.

And so another Warwick Farm race meeting concluded. We witnessed the usual air of efficiency plus all the "top" drivers, the latest in machinery and good close racing of a high standard. In fact, all combined to make this day worthy of its Interna-tional status — plus of course the Australian Grand Prix.

# JACK BRABHAM

*The victor stands under a gracious smile while the band plays "God Save the Queen."*

AS THE LITTLE GREEN COOPER swept along the Promenade at Monte Carlo for the final lap, its driver, 31 year old Jack Brabham, was at last able to relax. He had just finished the hardest battle of his career and won the Grand Prix of Monaco, first *Grande Epreuve* of 1959.

When he stepped out of the car all Jack could say was "This has been my best race." It was a very good "best"; all the way he had fought hard against Stirling Moss driving Rob Walker's privately prepared Cooper-Climax and Jean Behra in a works Ferrari. This may very well be a vintage year for Jack Brabham, one of the few drivers who makes his living racing. He and American driver Masten Gregory will be the mainstay of the Cooper team.

Brabham came into racing quite by accident; in fact he was really talked into it by Johnny Schonberg, one-time American racing driver. The two were on their way to Darwin from Sydney during the summer of 1946 and to pass the time Schonberg related tales of his midget car racing days.

After returning to Sydney the two built a midget in Jack's modest workshop and Brabham, as driver, won a name for himself in the next 12 months by winning the New South Wales championship. He continued in speedway racing until 1951, taking the South Australian and Australian championships. He then turned to racing on the road, mostly hill climbs, first with the midget and later with an early Mark IV Cooper.

In 1953 Brabham had a real stroke of luck; with some financial help from the Redex Oil Company and his father, he was fortunate enough to be able to purchase a newly arrived Cooper-Bristol. This car really started him on the road to success. That same year, Brabham decided he must go to England just for one season and while over there visit some of the leading manufacturers. Now, four years later, the fascination of motor racing in Europe still has Jack in its clutches and only occasionally does he return to Australia for a brief spell.

When he first raced in England in 1955, Brabham's cornering technique was most unusual; in fact it was a legacy from his midget racing days. He got around quickly enough "by using full lock and lots of throttle," as he put it. Now he has developed a neater style which has been fast enough to take the lap record at Goodwood, Crystal Palace and Brands Hatch.

Of all Jack's successes a race in which he didn't quite succeed, the Monaco Grand Prix of 1957, is still regarded as one of his greatest. In this event he was to drive the very first Grand Prix Formula I Cooper, owned by Rob Walker and prepared jointly by Alf Francis and the Cooper works mechanics. Construction of the new engine, enlarged to 2 liters, was delayed; it arrived at the Cooper works at Surbiton only one week before race day.

The Cooper mechanics worked all night to install the engine and testing had to be confined to a brief run up the by-pass in the early hours of the morning; then the new machine was hastily loaded on a truck to catch the cross channel boat. It arrived in Monte Carlo just in time for the first practice at dawn on Thursday.

According to instructions, Jack was to take it gently for the first laps to see how the car behaved. All went well until Jack was told to speed up; coming into a bend near the Casino a front brake locked up, causing the car to slew around and hit the protecting sandbags with a bang. Brabham climbed out unhurt, ruefully surveying the front end of the car with dismay. The engine was apparently undamaged, but to his expert eye it was obvious the car could not be repaired in time for the race. Fortunately the works team had brought a spare Formula II chassis along and Cooper decided to transfer engines.

At the start of the race Brabham wisely decided to stay out of the mad scramble on the opening laps and it paid off for after 3 laps Moss, Collins and Hawthorn were eliminated in a multiple pile-up.

Now as the race began to sort itself out Brabham gradually picked his way through the field and by the time one third of the race had been run he lay in fourth place, much to the delight of the huge crowd. The little Cooper gave away 500 cubic centimeters displacement to every other car in the race and spectators showed their admiration for its Australian driver who had calmly worked his way into third place 10 laps from the finish.

Then it happened. His car stuttered and came to a standstill with only 3 laps to go, his fuel pump drive sheared. Jack quickly realized he could still rank as a finisher if he pushed his car to the line one mile away. That mile was the longest Jack Brabham has ever known.

At the finish line an exhausted Brabham collapsed across his car, unable to speak or hear any of the applause. But his tremendous efforts laid the foundations of a new Formula I team that went on to win the Monaco Grand Prix the next year and again this year.

Jack Brabham has certainly developed into one of the world's top ranking drivers during his three and a half years of motor racing in Europe and his start this year marks him as a driver to watch.

# BRABHAM - ENTRIES AND PRACTICE TIMES OF BRABHAM RACING ORGANISATION LTD

| DATE | EVENT | DRIVER | CAR | PRACTICE TIMES 1 | PRACTICE TIMES 2 | PRACTICE TIMES 3 |
|---|---|---|---|---|---|---|
| 2 January 1967 | South African Grand Prix | J. Brabham | REPcoV8 | 1' 28.3" | - | 1'28.5" |
| 2 January 1967 | South African Grand Prix | D. Hulme | REPcoV8 | 1' 30.6" | 1' 28.8" | 1' 29.9" |
| 7 May 1967 | Monaco Grand Prix | J. Brabham | REPcoV8 | 1' 34.0" | 1'39.5" | 1' 27.6" |
| 7 May 1967 | Monaco Grand Prix | D. Hulme | REPcoV8 | 1' 30.2" | 1' 29.9" | 1. 28.8" |
| 4 June 1967 | Dutch Grand Prix | J. Brabham | REPcoV8 | 1' 29.1" | 1' 29.7" | 1' 27.1" |
| 4 June 1967 | Dutch Grand Prix | D. Hulme | REPcoV8 | 1' 26.8" | - | 1'26.8" |
| 18 June 1967 | Belgian Grand Prix | J. Brabham | REPcoV8 | 3' 36.9" | 3' 35.0" | |
| 18 June 1967 | Belgian Grand Prix | D. Hulme | REPcoV8 | 5' 57.9" | 3' 40.3" | |
| 2 July 1967 | French Grand Prix | J. Brabham | REPcoV8 | 1' 37.9" | 1' 36.3" | |
| 2 July 1967 | French Grand Prix | D. Hulme | REPcoV8 | 1' 38.0" | 1' 37.9" | |
| 15 July 1967 | British Grand Prix | J. Brabham | REPcoV8 | 1' 26.6" | 1' 27.7" | 1' 26.2" |
| 15 July 1967 | British Grand Prix | D. Hulme | REPcoV8 | 1' 27.6" | 1' 27.9" | 1' 26.3" |
| 6 August 1967 | German Grand Prix | J. Brabham | REPcoV8 | 9' 03.5" | 8' 18.9" | 8' 18.9" |
| 6 August 1967 | German Grand Prix | D. Hulme | REPcoV8 | 8' 25.4" | 8' 13.5" | 8' 13.5" |
| 27 August 1967 | Canadian Grand Prix | J. Brabham | REPcoV8 | 1' 24.7" | 1' 25.0" | - |
| 27 August 1967 | Canadian Grand Prix | D. Hulme | REPcoV8 | 1' 23.6" | 1' 23.2" | - |
| 10 September 1967 | Italian Grand Prix | J. Brabham | REPcoV8 | 1' 29.3" | 1' 28.8" | - |
| 10 September 1967 | Italian Grand Prix | D. Hulme | REPcoV8 | 1' 31.6" | 1' 29.4" | - |
| 1 October 1967 | United States Grand Prix | J. Brabham | REPcoV8 | 1' 21.60" | 1' 06.73" | - |

# BRABHAM - ENTRIES AND PRACTICE TIMES OF BRABHAM RACING ORGANISATION LTD

| DATE | EVENT | DRIVER | CAR | PRACTICE TIMES 1 | PRACTICE TIMES 2 | PRACTICE TIMES 3 |
|---|---|---|---|---|---|---|
| 1 October 1967 | United States Grand Prix | D. Hulme | REPcoV8 | 1' 08.09" | 1' 07.45" | - |
| 22 October 1967 | Mexican Grand Prix | J. Brabham | REPcoV8 | 1' 50.90" | 1' 49.08" | - |
| 22 October 1967 | Mexican Grand Prix | D. Hulme | REPcoV8 | 1' 49.79" | 1' 49.46 | - |
| 1 January 1968 | South African Grand Prix | J. Brabham | REPcoV8 | 1'26.7" | 1' 24.8" | 1' 23.2" |
| 1 January 1968 | South African Grand Prix | J. Rindt | REPcoV8 | 1'29.2" | 1' 25.2" | 1' 23.0" |
| 12 May 1968 | Spanish Grand Prix | J. Brabham | REPcoV8 | - | - | 1' 44.2" |
| 12 May 1968 | Spanish Grand Prix | J. Rindt | REPcoV8 | - | 1' 29.7" | 1' 29.7" |
| 26 May 1968 | Monaco Grand Prix | J. Brabham | REPcoV8 | - | 1' 31.2" | 1' 31.6" |
| 26 May 1968 | Monaco Grand Prix | J. Rindt | REPcoV8 | 1' 29.7" | 1' 29.2" | 1' 29.8" |
| 9 June 1968 | Belgian Grand Prix | J. Brabham | REPcoV8 | - | - | - |
| 9 June 1968 | Belgian Grand Prix | J. Rindt | REPcoV8 | 8' 04.0" | 4' 46.7" | - |
| 23 June 1968 | Dutch Grand Prix | J. Brabham | REPcoV8 | - | 1' 23.90" | 1' 47.22" |
| 23 June 1968 | Dutch Grand Prix | J. Rindt | | - | 1' 23.75" | 1' 23.70" |
| 7 July 1968 | French Grand Prix | J. Rindt | | 1' 56.1" | 2' 00.7" | - |
| 7 July 1968 | French Grand Prix | J. Brabham | | 2' 03.5" | 2' 00.8" | - |
| 20 July 1968 | British Grand Prix | J. Brabham | | 1' 37.7" | - | 1' 30.2" |
| 20 July 1968 | British Grand Prix | J. Rindt | | 1' 31.4" | 1' 31.8" | 1' 29.9" |
| 4 August 1968 | German Grand Prix | J. Brabham | | 10' 38.4" | 10' 23.1" | 10' 40.4" |
| 4 August 1968 | German Grand Prix | J. Rindt | | 9' 31.9" | 10' 13.9" | 10' 38.7" |

# BRABHAM - ENTRIES AND PRACTICE TIMES OF BRABHAM RACING ORGANISATION LTD

| DATE | EVENT | DRIVER | CAR | PRACTICE TIMES 1 | PRACTICE TIMES 2 | PRACTICE TIMES 3 |
|---|---|---|---|---|---|---|
| 8 September 1968 | Italian Grand Prix | J. Brabham | | 1' 28.8" | 1' 30.9" | - |
| 8 September 1968 | Italian Grand Prix | J. Rindt | | 1' 27.3" | 1' 29.7" | - |
| 22 September 1968 | Canadian Grand Prix | J. Brabham | | 1' 35.4" | 1' 35.8" | - |
| 22 September 1968 | Canadian Grand Prix | J. Rindt | | 1' 35.8" | 1' 33.8" | - |
| 6 October 1968 | United States Grand Prix | J. Brabham | REPcoV8 | 1' 06.22" | 1' 05.25" | - |
| 6 October 1968 | United States Grand Prix | J. Rindt | REPcoV8 | 1' 05.42" | 1' 04.81" | - |
| 3 November 1968 | Mexican Grand Prix | J. Brabham | REPcoV8 | 1' 50.30" | 1' 46.80" | - |
| 3 November 1968 | Mexican Grand Prix | J. Rindt | REPcoV8 | 1' 49.16" | 1' 47.07" | - |
| 1 March 1969 | South African Grand Prix | J. Brabham | BT26 | 1' 21.3" | 1' 20.0" | 1' 26.0" |
| 1 March 1969 | South African Grand Prix | J. Ickx | BT26 | 1' 25.0" | 1' 23.1" | 1' 24.1" |
| 4 May 1969 | Spanish Grand Prix | J. Brabham | BT26 | 1' 30.4" | 1' 32.3" | 1. 27.8" |
| 4 May 1969 | Spanish Grand Prix | J. Ickx | BT26 | - | 1' 30.0" | 1' 28.4" |
| 8 June 1969 | Monaco Grand Prix | J. Brabham | BT26 | 1' 31.0" | 1' 26.4" | 1' 26.5" |
| 8 June 1969 | Monaco Grand Prix | J. Ickx | BT26 | 1' 26.0" | 1' 26.3" | 1' 26.6" |
| 21 June 1969 | Dutch Grand Prix | J. Brabham | BT26 | 1' 24.34" | 1' 24.58" | 1' 23.10" |
| 21 June 1969 | Dutch Grand Prix | J. Ickx | BT26 | 1' 23.87" | 1' 24.00" | 1' 22.85" |
| 6 July 1969 | French Grand Prix | J. Ickx | BT26 | 3' 26.4" | 3' 05.9" | 3' 02.6" |
| 19 July 1969 | British Grand Prix | J. Ickx | BT26 | 1' 24.7" | - | 1' 28.8" |
| 3 August 1969 | German Grand Prix | J. Ickx | BT26 | 8' 33.8" | 7' 44.2" | 7' 42.1" |

# BRABHAM - ENTRIES AND PRACTICE TIMES OF BRABHAM RACING ORGANISATION LTD

| DATE | EVENT | DRIVER | CAR | PRACTICE TIMES 1 | PRACTICE TIMES 2 | PRACTICE TIMES 3 |
|---|---|---|---|---|---|---|
| 8 September 1969 | Italian Grand Prix | J. Brabham | BT26 | 1' 26.90" | 1' 27.10" | - |
| 8 September 1969 | Italian Grand Prix | J. Ickx | BT26 | 1' 37.96" | 2' 14.65" | - |
| 20 September 1969 | Canadian Grand Prix | J. Brabham | BT26 | 1' 18.0" | 1' 19.0" | - |
| 20 September 1969 | Canadian Grand Prix | J. Ickx | BT26 | 1' 18.3" | 1' 17.4" | - |
| 5 October 1969 | United States Grand Prix | J. Ickx | BT26 | 1' 14.24" | 1' 4.32" | - |
| 5 October 1969 | United States Grand Prix | J. Brabham | BT26 | 1' 13.84" | 1' 4.80" | - |
| 19 October 1969 | Mexican Grand Prix | J. Ickx | BT26 | 1' 43.60" | 1' 43.86" | - |
| 19 October 1969 | Mexican Grand Prix | J. Brabham | BT26 | 1' 42.90" | 1. 44.67" | - |
| 7 March 1970 | South African Grand Prix | J. Brabham | BT33 | 1' 20.2" | 1' 19.6" | 1' 20.0" |
| 19 April 1970 | Spanish Grand Prix | J. Brabham | BT33 | 1' 24.5" | 1' 24.6" | 1' 23.9" |
| 10 May 1970 | Monaco Grand Prix | J. Brabham | BT33 | 1' 25.8" | 1' 43.1" | 1' 25.4" |
| 7 June 1970 | Belgian Grand Prix | J. Brabham | BT33 | 3' 31.5" | 3' 45.0" | 3' 32.9" |
| 21 June 1970 | Dutch Grand Prix | J. Brabham | BT33 | 1' 21.19" | 1' 20.76" | 1' 20.83" |
| 5 July 1970 | French Grand Prix | J. Brabham | BT33 | 3' 07.06" | 3' 04.00" | 2' 59.67" |
| 18 July 1970 | British Grand Prix | J. Brabham | BT33 | 1' 26.6" | 1' 24.8" | - |
| 2 August 1970 | German Grand Prix | J. Brabham | BT33 | 2' 02.3" | 2' 02.0" | 2' 02.0" |
| 16 August 1970 | Austrian Grand Prix | J. Brabham | BT33 | 1' 43.40" | 1' 42.20" | 1' 40.81" |
| 8 September 1970 | Italian Grand Prix | J. Brabham | BT33 | 1' 26.61" | 1' 26.37" | 1' 25.39" |
| 20 September 1970 | Canadian Grand Prix | J. Brabham | BT33 | 1' 46.8" | 1' 35.5" | 1' 35.4" |

# BRABHAM - ENTRIES AND PRACTICE TIMES OF BRABHAM RACING ORGANISATION LTD

| DATE | EVENT | DRIVER | CAR | PRACTICE TIMES 1 | PRACTICE TIMES 2 | PRACTICE TIMES 3 |
|---|---|---|---|---|---|---|
| 4 October 1970 | United States Grand Prix | J. Brabham | BT33 | 1' 05.29" | 1' 16.74" | - |
| 18 October 1970 | Mexican Grand Prix | J. Brabham | BT33 | 1' 43.92" | 1' 43.57" | - |
| 6 March 1971 | South African Grand Prix | G. Hill | BT33 | 1' 20.7" | 1' 20.5" | 1' 21.1" |
| 6 March 1971 | South African Grand Prix | D. Charlton | BT33 | 1' 21.1" | 1' 20.8" | 1' 19.8" |
| 18 April 1971 | Spanish Grand Prix | G. Hill | BT34 | 1' 28.4" | 1' 30.3" | 1' 43.4" |
| 18 April 1971 | Spanish Grand Prix | T. Schenken | BT33 | 1' 32.3" | 1' 30.6" | 1' 43.1" |
| 23 May 1971 | Monaco Grand Prix | G. Hill | BT34 | 1' 50.1" | 1' 26.0" | 1' 40.7" |
| 23 May 1971 | Monaco Grand Prix | T. Schenken | BT33 | - | 1' 28.3" | 1' 40.2" |
| 20 June 1971 | Dutch Grand Prix | G. Hill | BT34 | 1' 20.07" | 1' 42.31" | 1' 21.06" |
| 20 June 1971 | Dutch Grand Prix | T. Schenken | BT34 | 1' 20.35" | 1' 43.53" | 1' 22.13" |
| 4 July 1971 | French Grand Prix | G. Hill | BT34 | 1' 56.03" | 1' 54.35" | 1' 52.32" |
| 4 July 1971 | French Grand Prix | T. Schenken | BT33 | 1' 55.43" | 1' 53.58" | 1' 55.13" |
| 17 July 1971 | British Grand Prix | G. Hill | BT34 | 1' 21.0" | 1' 20.3" | 1' 31.7" |
| 17 July 1971 | British Grand Prix | T. Schenken | BT33 | 1' 21.1" | 1' 20.3" | 1' 19.89" |
| 1 August 1971 | German Grand Prix | G. Hill | BT34 | 7' 39.6" | 7. 36.1" | 7' 38.9" |
| 1 August 1971 | German Grand Prix | T. Schenken | BT33 | 7' 49.2" | 7' 37.2" | 7' 29.8" |
| 15 August 1971 | Austrian Grand Prix | G. Hill | BT34 | 1' 43.72" | 1' 39.55" | 1' 38.70" |
| 15 August 1971 | Austrian Grand Prix | T. Schenken | BT33 | 1' 39.75" | 1' 38.90" | 1' 38.64" |
| 5 September 1971 | Italian Grand Prix | G. Hill | BT34 | 1' 25.05" | - | 1' 24.27" |

# BRABHAM - ENTRIES AND PRACTICE TIMES OF BRABHAM RACING ORGANISATION LTD

| DATE | EVENT | DRIVER | CAR | PRACTICE TIMES 1 | PRACTICE TIMES 2 | PRACTICE TIMES 3 |
|---|---|---|---|---|---|---|
| 5 September 1971 | Italian Grand Prix | T. Schenken | BT33 | 1' 25.34" | - | 1' 23.73" |
| 19 September 1971 | Canadian Grand Prix | T. Schenken | BT33 | 1' 21.6" | 1' 17.9" | 1' 17.4" |
| 19 September 1971 | Canadian Grand Prix | G. Hill | BT34 | 1' 21.1" | 1' 17.2" | 1' 17.2" |
| 3 October 1971 | United States Grand Prix | G. Hill | BT34 | 1' 47.480" | 1' 45.448" | - |
| 3 October 1971 | United States Grand Prix | T. Schenken | BT34 | 1' 45.110" | 1' 46.702" | - |
| 3 October 1971 | United States Grand Prix | C. Craft | BT33 | 1' 49.421" | 1' 48.698" | - |
| 23 January 1972 | Argentine Grand Prix | G. Hill | BT33 | 1' 16.34" | 1' 14.52" | - |
| 23 January 1972 | Argentine Grand Prix | C. Reutemann | BT34 | 1' 14.71" | 1' 12.46" | - |
| 4 March 1972 | South African Grand Prix | G. Hill | BT33 | 1' 18.6" | 1' 18.2" | 1' 18.1" |
| 4 March 1972 | South African Grand Prix | C. Reutemann | BT34 | 1' 18.8" | 1' 18.2" | 1' 18.3" |
| 1 May 1972 | Spanish Grand Prix | G. Hill | BT37 | 1' 23.70" | 1' 22.59" | - |
| 1 May 1972 | Spanish Grand Prix | W. Fittipaldi | BT33 | 1' 21.49" | 1. 20.83" | - |
| 14 May 1972 | Monaco Grand Prix | G. Hill | BT37 | - | 1' 24.7" | 1' 53.3" |
| 14 May 1972 | Monaco Grand Prix | W. Fittipaldi | BT33 | 1' 26.2" | 1' 25.2" | - |
| 4 June 1972 | Belgian Grand Prix | G. Hill | BT37 | 1' 14.7" | 1' 14.3" | 1' 13.1" |
| 4 June 1972 | Belgian Grand Prix | W. Fittipaldi | BT34 | 1' 13.2" | 1' 13.6" | 1' 13.8" |
| 4 June 1972 | Belgian Grand Prix | C. Reutemann | BT37 | 1' 13.2" | 1. 12.5" | 1. 12.56" |
| 4 July 1972 | French Grand Prix | G. Hill | BT37 | 3' 3.0" | 3' 3.2" | 3' 4.2" |
| 4 July 1972 | French Grand Prix | W. Fittipaldi | BT34 | 3' 2.4" | 2' 59.5" | 3' 22.3" |

# BRABHAM - ENTRIES AND PRACTICE TIMES OF BRABHAM RACING ORGANISATION LTD

| DATE | EVENT | DRIVER | CAR | PRACTICE TIMES 1 | PRACTICE TIMES 2 | PRACTICE TIMES 3 |
|---|---|---|---|---|---|---|
| 4 July 1972 | French Grand Prix | C. Reutemann | BT37 | 3' 0.7" | 3' 3.8" | 3' 11.7" |
| 17 July 1972 | European Grand Prix | G. Hill | BT37 | 1' 26.1" | 1' 26.5" | 1' 25.2" |
| 17 July 1972 | European Grand Prix | C. Reutemann | BT37 | 1' 26.2" | 1' 24.7" | 1' 23.8" |
| 17 July 1972 | European Grand Prix | W. Fittipaldi | BT34 | 1' 26.4" | 1' 26.3" | 1' 26.4" |
| 1 August 1972 | German Grand Prix | G. Hill | BT37 | 7' 42.9" | 7' 33.6" | 7' 18.4" |
| 1 August 1972 | German Grand Prix | C. Reutemann | BT37 | 7' 47.9" | 7' 18.7" | 7' 12.4" |
| 1 August 1972 | German Grand Prix | W. Fittipaldi | BT34 | 7' 31.1" | 7' 24.8" | 7' 27.1" |
| 13 August 1972 | Austrian Grand Prix | G. Hill | BT37 | 1' 38.14" | 1' 39.05" | - |
| 13 August 1972 | Austrian Grand Prix | C. Reutemann | BT37 | 1' 40.53" | 1' 37.15" | - |
| 13 August 1972 | Austrian Grand Prix | W. Fittipaldi | BT34 | 1' 40.53" | 1' 38.25" | - |
| 10 September 1972 | Italian Grand Prix | G. Hill | BT37 | 1' 38.71" | 1' 37.61" | - |
| 10 September 1972 | Italian Grand Prix | W. Fittipaldi | BT34 | 1' 38.35" | 1' 37.82" | - |
| 10 September 1972 | Italian Grand Prix | C. Reutemann | BT37 | 1' 38.42" | 1' 37.12" | - |
| 24 September 1972 | Canadian Grand Prix | G. Hill | BT37 | 1' 21.7" | 1' 19.7" | 1' 16.2" |
| 24 September 1972 | Canadian Grand Prix | C. Reutemann | BT37 | 1' 17.5" | 1' 15.7" | 1' 14.9" |
| 24 September 1972 | Canadian Grand Prix | W. Fittipaldi | BT34 | 1' 16.6" | 1' 16.0" | 1' 15.6" |
| 8 October 1972 | United States Grand Prix | G. Hill | BT37 | 1' 46.31" | 2' 9.76" | 2' 6.25" |
| 8 October 1972 | United States Grand Prix | C. Reutemann | BT37 | 1' 41.69" | 2' 8.27" | 2' 5.17" |
| 8 October 1972 | United States Grand Prix | W. Fittipaldi | BT34 | 1' 42.76" | - | 2' 4.17" |

# BRABHAM - ENTRIES AND PRACTICE TIMES OF BRABHAM RACING ORGANISATION LTD

| DATE | EVENT | DRIVER | CAR | PRACTICE TIMES 1 | PRACTICE TIMES 2 | PRACTICE TIMES 3 |
|---|---|---|---|---|---|---|
| 28 January 1973 | Argentine Grand Prix | C. Reutemann | BT37 | 1' 13.49" | 1' 12.66" | 1' 15.24" |
| 28 January 1973 | Argentine Grand Prix | W. Fittipaldi | BT37 | 1' 14.06" | 1' 13.78" | 1' 13.04" |
| 11 February 1973 | Brazilian Grand Prix | C. Reutemann | BT37 | 2' 34.6" | 2' 32.9" | 2' 34.6" |
| 11 February 1973 | Brazilian Grand Prix | W. Fittipaldi | BT37 | 2' 35.9" | 2' 34.3" | 2' 36.4" |
| 3 March 1973 | South African Grand Prix | C. Reutemann | BT37 | 1' 17.66" | 1' 16.94" | 1' 17.33" |
| 3 March 1973 | South African Grand Prix | W. Fittipaldi | BT37 | 1' 19.11" | 1' 17.95" | 1' 18.17" |
| 29 April 1973 | Spanish Grand Prix | W. Fittipaldi | BT42 | 1' 26.1" | 1' 26.1" | 1' 24.5" |
| 29 April 1973 | Spanish Grand Prix | C. Reutemann | BT42 | 1' 36.2" | 1' 25.9" | 1' 24.7" |
| 20 May 1973 | European Grand Prix | C. Reutemann | BT42 | 1' 28.05" | 1' 23.85" | 1' 23.34" |
| 20 May 1973 | European Grand Prix | W. Fittipaldi | BT42 | 1' 32.89" | 1' 26.06" | 1' 25.51" |
| 3 June 1973 | Monaco Grand Prix | C. Reutemann | BT42 | 1' 31.9" | 1' 31.8" | 1' 30.1" |
| 3 June 1973 | Monaco Grand Prix | W. Fittipaldi | BT42 | 1' 31.5" | 1' 30.8" | 1' 28.9" |
| 17 June 1973 | Swedish Grand Prix | C. Reutemann | BT42 | 1' 25.08" | 1' 24.48" | - |
| 17 June 1973 | Swedish Grand Prix | W. Fittipaldi | BT42 | - | 1' 27.05" | 1' 26.12" |
| 1 July 1973 | French Grand Prix | C. Reutemann | BT42 | 1' 53.45" | 1' 50.75" | 1' 50.88" |
| 1 July 1973 | French Grand Prix | W. Fittipaldi | BT42 | 1' 52.14" | 1' 52.43" | 1' 52.07" |
| 14 July 1973 | British Grand Prix | C. Reutemann | BT42 | 1' 17.9" | 1' 17.4" | - |
| 14 July 1973 | British Grand Prix | W. Fittipaldi | BT42 | 1' 18.5" | 1' 18.1" | - |
| 29 July 1973 | Dutch Grand Prix | C. Reutemann | BT42 | 1' 36.37" | - | 1' 23.13" |

# BRABHAM - ENTRIES AND PRACTICE TIMES OF BRABHAM RACING ORGANISATION LTD

| DATE | EVENT | DRIVER | CAR | PRACTICE TIMES 1 | PRACTICE TIMES 2 | PRACTICE TIMES 3 |
|---|---|---|---|---|---|---|
| 29 July 1973 | Dutch Grand Prix | W. Fittipaldi | BT42 | - | - | 1' 22.76" |
| 5 August 1973 | German Grand Prix | C. Reutemann | BT42 | 7' 15.1" | 7' 25.3" | - |
| 5 August 1973 | German Grand Prix | W. Fittipaldi | BT42 | 7' 21.4" | 7' 19.1" | - |
| 19 August 1973 | Austrian Grand Prix | R. Stommelen | BT42 | 1' 40.53" | - | - |
| 19 August 1973 | Austrian Grand Prix | C. Reutemann | BT42 | 1' 37.5" | 1' 36.01" | 1' 36.29" |
| 19 August 1973 | Austrian Grand Prix | W. Fittipaldi | BT42 | 1' 38.43" | - | - |
| 9 September 1973 | Italian Grand Prix | R. Stommelen | BT42 | - | 1' 38.03" | 1' 36.54" |
| 9 September 1973 | Italian Grand Prix | C. Reutemann | BT42 | - | 1' 37.81" | 1' 36.55" |
| 9 September 1973 | Italian Grand Prix | W. Fittipaldi | BT42 | - | 1' 38.4" | 1' 38.23" |
| 23 September 1973 | Canadian Grand Prix | R. Stommelen | BT42 | 1' 16.84" | 1' 16.99" | 1' 27.02" |
| 23 September 1973 | Canadian Grand Prix | C. Reutemann | BT42 | 1' 15.48" | 1' 14.81" | 1' 15.83" |
| 23 September 1973 | Canadian Grand Prix | W. Fittipaldi | BT42 | 1' 17.79" | 1' 16.11" | 1' 16.15" |
| 7 October 1973 | United States Grand Prix | J. Watson | BT42 | 1' 44.45" | 1' 43.88" | 1' 44.08" |
| 7 October 1973 | United States Grand Prix | C. Reutemann | BT42 | 1' 41.36" | 1' 40.01" | 1' 41.4" |
| 7 October 1973 | United States Grand Prix | W. Fittipaldi | BT42 | 1' 45.57" | 1' 52.91" | 1' 44.47" |
| 13 January 1974 | Argentine Grand Prix | C. Reutemann | BT44 | 1' 54.81" | 1' 51.55" | 1' 53.69" |
| 13 January 1974 | Argentine Grand Prix | R. Robarts | BT44 | - | 1' 55.98" | 1' 57.00" |
| 27 January 1974 | Brazilian Grand Prix | C. Reutemann | BT44 | 2' 34.63" | 2' 34.09" | 2' 33.21" |
| 27 January 1974 | Brazilian Grand Prix | R. Robarts | BT44 | 2' 44.39" | 2' 41.73" | 2' 40.82" |

# BRABHAM - ENTRIES AND PRACTICE TIMES OF BRABHAM RACING ORGANISATION LTD

| DATE | EVENT | DRIVER | CAR | PRACTICE TIMES 1 | PRACTICE TIMES 2 | PRACTICE TIMES 3 |
|---|---|---|---|---|---|---|
| 30 March 1974 | South African Grand Prix | C. Reutemann | BT44 | 1' 16.80" | 1' 17.15" | - |
| 30 March 1974 | South African Grand Prix | R. Robarts | BT44 | 1' 18.80" | 1' 18.60" | - |
| 28 April 1974 | Spanish Grand Prix | C. Reutemann | BT44 | 1' 19.37" | 1' 19.84" | 1' 19.37" |
| 28 April 1974 | Spanish Grand Prix | R. von Opel | BT44 | 1' 27.87" | 1' 24.54" | 1' 22.96" |
| 12 May 1974 | Belgian Grand Prix | C. Reutemann | BT44 | - | 1' 26.20" | 1' 17.11" |
| 12 May 1974 | Belgian Grand Prix | R. von Opel | BT44 | 1' 22.87" | 1' 19.92" | 1' 13.61" |
| 26 May 1974 | Monaco Grand Prix | C. Reutemann | BT44 | 1' 31.0" | 1' 28.8" | 1' 27.8" |
| 9 June 1974 | Swedish Grand Prix | C. Reutemann | BT44 | - | - | 1' 26.85" |
| 9 June 1974 | Swedish Grand Prix | R. von Opel | BT44 | 1' 30.99" | 1' 33.78" | 1' 27.69" |
| 23 June 1974 | Dutch Grand Prix | C. Reutemann | BT44 | 1' 21.81" | 1' 20.50" | 1' 22.16" |
| 23 June 1974 | Dutch Grand Prix | R. von Opel | BT44 | 1' 23.30" | 1' 23.19" | 1' 21.56" |
| 7 July 1974 | French Grand Prix | C. Reutemann | BT44 | 59.33" | 59.84" | 59.80" |
| 20 July 1974 | British Grand Prix | C. Pace | BT44 | 1'23.0" | 1' 22.3" | 1' 21.7" |
| 20 July 1974 | British Grand Prix | C. Reutemann | BT44 | 1' 21.9" | 1' 21.9" | 1' 20.6" |
| 4 August 1974 | German Grand Prix | C. Reutemann | BT44 | 7' 7.2" | 7' 13.4" | - |
| 4 August 1974 | German Grand Prix | C. Pace | BT44 | - | 7' 12.7" | - |
| 18 August 1974 | Austrian Grand Prix | C. Reutemann | BT44 | 1' 36.61" | 1' 35.56" | 1' 38.92" |
| 18 August 1974 | Austrian Grand Prix | C. Pace | BT44 | 1' 37.02" | - | 1' 35.91" |
| 8 September 1974 | Italian Grand Prix | C. Reutemann | BT44 | 1' 33.64" | 1' 33.27" | - |

# BRABHAM - ENTRIES AND PRACTICE TIMES OF BRABHAM RACING ORGANISATION LTD

| DATE | EVENT | DRIVER | CAR | PRACTICE TIMES 1 | PRACTICE TIMES 2 | PRACTICE TIMES 3 |
|---|---|---|---|---|---|---|
| 8 September 1974 | Italian Grand Prix | C. Pace | BT44 | 1' 34.80" | 1' 34.06" | 1' 33.53" |
| 22 September 1974 | Canadian Grand Prix | C. Reutemann | BT44 | 1' 14.2" | 1' 13.74" | 1' 15.12" |
| 22 September 1974 | Canadian Grand Prix | C. Pace | BT44 | 1' 14.1" | 1' 14.19" | 1' 14.10" |
| 6 October 1974 | United States Grand Prix | C. Reutemann | BT44 | 1' 39.27" | 1' 39.29" | 1' 39.64" |
| 6 October 1974 | United States Grand Prix | C. Pace | BT44 | 1' 39.88" | 1' 39.28" | 1' 40.54" |

# Jack Brabham

## He's 21 (in motor racing) this year, and determined to celebrate

After picking up a couple of the £100 bonuses during practice for the Daily Express Trophy at Silverstone, Jack Brabham remarked wryly that this was more than he earned during the whole of 1968. Stretching it a bit, perhaps, because he does derive a modest income from making scores of race-winning single-seaters and from owning garages at Chessington and Worcester Park. Modest enough, that is, to be able to own his own plane and a very pleasant lawn-surrounded house backing on to a Surrey golf course.

But 1968 was one of Jack's low seasons. After those tremendous successes of 1966 and 1967, when he picked up his third world championship and then provided Denny with the car which gave him the title, he went through last season with virtually nothing to show for his Grand Prix effort except two points for fifth place in the German GP. That plus a load of worry, days and days of round-the-clock work, and repeated mechanical failures with his twin-cam Repco V8 engines.

Yet through it all this engaging Australian, who has now reached the stage when he no longer winces when someone mentions his age, never gave the slightest outward hint that he had any worries at all. He could always raise a smile, joke about his misfortune . . . then get back to the job of trying to get things right.

If ever John Arthur Brabham decides to take up poker then some of the experts will have to look to their bank balances. He conceals his feelings behind a broad grin, and does it win or lose. And he plays his cards mighty close to his chest. Perhaps you will recall how, late in 1965, he was blithely telling people that he might have to give up Grand Prix racing when the 3 litre formula began, and all the while he was popping over to Melbourne to discuss progress on the Repco V8 with single overhead cams.

That was one of Jack's shrewdest decisions, and one of his best-kept secrets. Choosing a modest power unit with bags of torque in a simple, light chassis that had probably the best roadholding of any rival at the time, was a master stroke at that stage.

The real pay-off came at Reims that year, when Jack became the first driver to win a Grand Prix in a car of his own construction. Even now, he considers it his proudest race moment, yet shortly after taking the winner's wreath he was leaning over the rails in the paddock, intent on seeing one of his F3 cars win the supporting event. That gives a clue to his success; he just never lets up.

Last year there must have been moments when he wondered whether Formula 1 really was worthwhile. Indeed, he did give careful thought to the idea of pulling out at the end of last season. Then he thought again, and argued that his record in 1968 was so awful that he simply had to do something about it this year. So he swopped over to Ford-Cosworth V8s, made a few modifications to last year's F1 design, and promptly snatched pole position for the South African GP.

Jack's smile got broader at Kyalami, and even when he had to retire following 'wing' trouble during the race, he was not disheartened. He knew then that he had the recipe that might give him the chance of a fourth world championship.

The morale graph took a bit of a tumble at the Race of Champions, when both Jack and Jacky Ickx had to retire, but they came storming back at Silverstone, with first and fourth respectively. It was Jack's first F1 victory since the Canadian GP of 1967. Then, instead of resting on his laurels, he rushed over to the other side of the world and the next weekend won a Tasman formula race at Bathurst.

He's now 43, and this is his 21st season in motoring competition, yet all his rivals are agreed that Black Jack (how he got that nickname no one seems to know) is driving as well, if not better, than ever. His style has matured since 1955, when he first made the trek from Sydney to Britain; his cinder track career came through very clearly at that time as he managed to have the back end of his car hanging further out on the corners than anyone else. The crowds loved it, and it was then the only way Jack knew to get round the bends. Now he performs more stylishly, though vigorously, yet when he's really under pressure the trackside grass begins to ruffle . . . and he's a very difficult chap to overtake.

Some of Jack's GP rivals swear that he never takes a corner the same way twice. Maybe not, but he gets results, and that's what counts.

Indeed, Jack is extremely thoughtful about his driving. Times, he says, have definitely changed, and whereas in former years a driver could get success with skill and bags of courage, nowadays victories only come from an intelligent application to the job. He says, 'To win races these days you have to think, and never stop thinking'.

This is where experience pays off, and Jack has plenty of that. He demonstrated it at Silverstone where, under treacherous conditions, he had the measure of everyone else. It was not, however, merely his driver experience, for Jack is the complete racing man. Probably no other driver has his ability for sorting a car to its maximum potential. Years of experience have given him an almost uncanny knack for putting his finger on a handling problem, and not only finding it but suggesting the solution as well. It goes even further than that, for he also has the practical ability to carry out the work with his own hands. That is probably why he commands such respect from his mechanics.

Behind the equable exterior of this quiet Australian is a relentless urge to win. It would be going too far to suggest that he is ruthless, but he really doesn't want to know anything except the chequered flag.

This sort of make-up often goes with a disdain for others that leads to unpopularity. Not with Jack. His rivals may fear him, but they also respect him. He can also reveal a sympathy and understanding for others that is oddly at variance with his dedication. Like that Saturday afternoon at Spa in 1960 when he was one of the first to get to the hospital where Stirling Moss had been taken after his dramatic accident. Or the morning before last year's French GP, when he handed over his considerable pre-race problems to his team while he flew back to England a friend with a desperate domestic problem.

There are quite a few racegoers who ask, 'Why does Jack go on racing?' After all, he has enough businesses to be able to settle back comfortably and watch his racing from the sidelines instead of in the cockpit.

The answer to that one is simple, and Jack says it simply. 'I just like racing', he says. 'I just like to be busy working on the development of a racing car, and I like competition. In fact, I can't imagine not being in motor racing.'

The time must come, of course, when he finally hangs up his helmet. (There were signs that he might have been thinking of this five or so years back.) At the moment, though, he's going as well as ever, and recalling that Fangio won the first of his five world championships when he was 40 (when Jack won his third), there's still time for this Sydneysider to get a nap hand of world titles.

What is certain is that it won't come through anything wildly revolutionary in the designs he works out with Ron Tauranac (the 'T' of the 'BT' in the Brabham type numbers). Between them they've got their results through sound, basic engineering; they never take chances on something which offers possibilities but which might prove fragile or unreliable. There is an innate conservatism about Jack which contrasts oddly with his undoubted adventurous spirit (remember he has piloted his own plane across the Atlantic and also to Australia). While everyone was madly following Colin Chapman's monocoque concept, Jack was content to stick to spaceframe chassis, because it produced sufficiently good results and had an added advantage of being cheaper to repair. Now he has opted for his first monocoque F1 car, which we'll see soon, and finally put the front suspension away out of the air stream.

In his work as a constructor, Jack makes haste slowly. In the cockpit he makes haste. His performances already this season give warning to his rivals that he again means business. With young Jacky Ickx as his team-mate he could be in for another good year. He doesn't seem too concerned about all these four-wheel-drive cars, either. Which suggests that he knows a thing or two. Or is he about to spring another Repco-type bluff on to the world of Grand Prix racing?

Trouble about Jack is that you never can tell what he's thinking. But don't be misled by that ever-present smile.

*Grid line-up—with Brabham (No. 2), Clark (No. 6) and Irwin (No. 4) on the front row, and Beltoise (No. 20) and Rindt (No. 36) behind them on the second*

# BRABHAM'S FINAL PROOF

*Virtually invincible in formula 2 racing, Jack Brabham and his Brabham-Honda go on their way to their ninth win this year—making doubly certain of the French Formula 2 Championship, which Brabham has added to his 1966 Drivers' World Championship*

JACK BRABHAM took one of his invincible formula 2 Brabham-Hondas to yet another victory in last Sunday's Grand Prix de France race at Albi. Backed up by Chris Irwin in the car usually driven by Denny Hulme, in third place, Brabham led comfortably for all but six laps to win the last race for 1,000 c.c. formula 2 cars in France. A fine drive by Jo Schlesser (Matra-Cosworth) was rewarded with second place after Beltoise had dropped out with throttle linkage trouble.

Albi is a pleasant rural town some 75 kilometres from Toulouse in southern France. As the formula 2 teams had already been in France for two weeks, with previous engagements at Montlhéry and Le Mans, the entry was a very good one, with all the usual teams less Trevor Taylor and Bob Anderson; they had gone home following their Le Mans shunt with Hobbs' M.R.P. Lola. However, the Lola team had rushed another monocoque chassis out, the original one, and made up one car from the bits of two for Frank Gardner to drive. The teams at Albi were therefore: Ron Harris (Jim Clark, Peter Arundell, Eric Offenstadt); Matra Sports (Jean-Pierre Beltoise, Jo Schlesser, Ludovico Scarfiotti); M.R.P. (Richard Attwood, Frank Gardner); Brabham Developments (Jack Brabham, Chris Irwin); Winkelmann Racing (Alan Rees, Jochen Rindt); Ken Tyrrell (Jackie Stewart, Jacky Ickx); John Coombs (Graham Hill); Caltex Racing (Kurt Ahrens) and Eric Offenstadt (Jean Rolland).

Practice was on Friday and Saturday, with most of the fast times being put up on the second day. Brabham got busy right from the word go and at the end of first practice was fastest in 1min 19·0sec from Rindt with 1min 19·8 sec—but neither Beltoise nor Schlesser practised. On Saturday Brabham's time came down to 1min 18·8sec, but Clark was challenging hard now with 1min 19·1sec, followed by Irwin (thanks to a tow by Jack right at the end) in 1min 19·2sec, Beltoise in 1min 19·4sec and Rindt and Schlesser with 1min 19·7sec each. Arundell was the only driver in serious trouble (with a broken valve) but his junior team-mate Offenstadt was not feeling at all well.

Race day brought over 40,000 fans, the blue sky and warm sun obviously helping. At the start Brabham jumped into the lead followed by Clark, Irwin, Beltoise, Schlesser and Rindt, with rally driver and Alpine winner Jean Rolland already dropping back in Offenstadt's Lola-B.R.M. Lap two and the first two places were the same but Beltoise had passed Irwin who, a lap later, was also passed by Rindt. Then on lap four the crowd went wild as Beltoise thrust in front of the Australian into the lead, and stayed there for the next five laps. Behind, Rindt was busily establishing himself at third while on lap 11 Irwin got past Clark, who had steadily dropped back after an initial second place.

On lap nine Brabham re-took the lead from the gallant Matra driver, but Beltoise never let up, worrying the Brabham's tail all the time.

Now the leaders began to spread out; Brabham, Beltoise and Rindt formed the leading trio with Irwin, Clark and Schlesser in the second. Clark was however quite obviously not happy and on lap 15 Schlesser passed him and began to pull away. Five laps later the Winkelmann team suffered a serious blow when they lost both cars on the same lap, Rindt with a blown engine and Rees with throttle linkage and valve trouble. Ahrens, too, had gone while Stewart's Matra-Cosworth had dropped a valve, and Scarfiotti given up in disgust with engine trouble. The order at 25 laps was Brabham, Beltoise, then a gap to Irwin and other gap to Schlesser, who was well clear of Arundell and Clark.

As the leaders maintained station a tremendous battle for seventh place developed between the two Lolas of M.R.P. and Ickx in Tyrrell's Matra-B.R.M. Clark was still in trouble, and soon he lost sixth place to the battling trio as his Lotus 44 stammered round the circuit. Now Arundell was in trouble, and as the field rapidly thinned so Arundell pulled up with a broken camshaft. Then when Offenstadt stopped, the Lotus rot had really set in, with Clark now eighth and falling back all the time.

With the race half run Beltoise still stayed fixed to Brabham's tail, although now a little farther back. Jack was however looking a little worried and one guessed that the wily old fox was holding quite a lot in hand. Clark was now in the pits, and the mechanics suspected fuel vaporization, but sent him off again at the tail of the field.

For a while there was little change, but Schlesser was closing on Irwin while Ickx, Gardner and Attwood were driving as though in a 10-lap race at Brands Hatch, so furious was their battle.

On lap 53 Schlesser finally passed Irwin, but Chris was suffering considerable vibration under braking, and although he re-passed Schlesser again, he was soon behind for good.

From laps 53 to 65 there was no change save for fifth place which altered sometimes three or four times a lap, with Ickx having the lion's share of the lead. Then on lap 66 Beltoise's engine suddenly stammered, and he coasted into the pits. For five laps he stood at the pits while mechanics repaired the throttle linkage, dropping him from second to eighth.

*Second and third men home—Schlesser's Matra-Cosworth leads Chris Irwin's Brabham-Honda, with signs of an excursion on to the dusty grass still in the air behind them!*

**Brabham Triumphant**

And so the race ran out with Brabham the undisputed winner, Schlesser a good second, Irwin third, then Ickx, Gardner and Attwood, the last having thrown a lot of oil out for many laps. In all there were 10 survivors from a field of 17. Brabham set a new lap record of 1min 19·3sec (103·82 m.p.h.).

The supporting formula 3 race was divided into two 25-lap heats with an aggregate result. Piers Courage won both in a Lotus 41, although bothered considerably in part one by Fenning's well-driven Tyrrell Matra. Fenning's engine was down on power in part two, and a lowly fifth place was the best he could do. This gave Jaussaud second overall in a works Matra with Vidal (Brabham) third, and Mo Nunn (Lotus 41) fourth. Derek Bell was sixth in his Lotus 41, while Widdows (Brabham) retired after a promising display.

Typical of the hotly contested formula 3 class, there was a hair-raising shunt on lap two of the first race when Roy Pike (Lucas Lotus 41) made a mistake and spun. John Cardwell (Ron Harris Lotus 41) leapt four feet in the air as his car cleared Pike's, while Blokdyk (Brabham) damaged his nose section. Somehow all three cars continued the race, which is rather remarkable in such circumstances. As in the formula 2 race, the lap record went again, to Courage in 1min 22·5sec (98·59 m.p.h.).

**RESULTS**

**(85 laps of 2·26-mile circuit: 192·10 miles)**
1. Brabham-Honda (J. Brabham). 1hr 54min 32·2sec, 100·60 m.p.h.;
2. Matra-Cosworth (J. Schlesser). 1hr 55min 04·1 sec;
3. Brabham-Honda (C. Irwin) 1hr 55min 04·3 sec;
4 Matra-B.R.M. (J. Ickx). 84 laps; 5. Lola-Cosworth (F. Gardner). 84 laps; 6 Lola-Cosworth (R Attwood). 83 laps; 7. Lola-B.R.M. (J. Rolland). 82 laps; 8. Matra-Cosworth (J.-P. Beltoise). 80 laps; 9 Lotus-Cosworth (J. Clark). 74 laps; 10. Matra-B R.M. (G. Hill). 68 laps;
**Fastest lap (new record):** J. Brabham (Brabham-Honda), 1min 19·3sec, 103·82 m.p.h.

**Formula 3: (2×25 laps of 2·26-mile circuit: 113 miles)**
1. Lotus-Ford (P. Courage) 1hr 09min 48.5sec. 97·09 m.p.h.;
2 Matra-Ford (J.-P Jaussaud). 1hr 10min 29·9sec;
3. Brabham-Ford (P. Vidal). 1hr 10min 36·4sec;
4. Lotus-Ford (M. Nunn) 1hr 10min 39·2sec; 5. Matra-Ford (J. Fenning); 6. Lotus-Ford (D. Bell);
**Fastest lap (new record):** P. Courage (Lotus-Ford), 1min 22·5sec, 98·59 m.p.h.

# BRABHAM'S NEW ENGINE

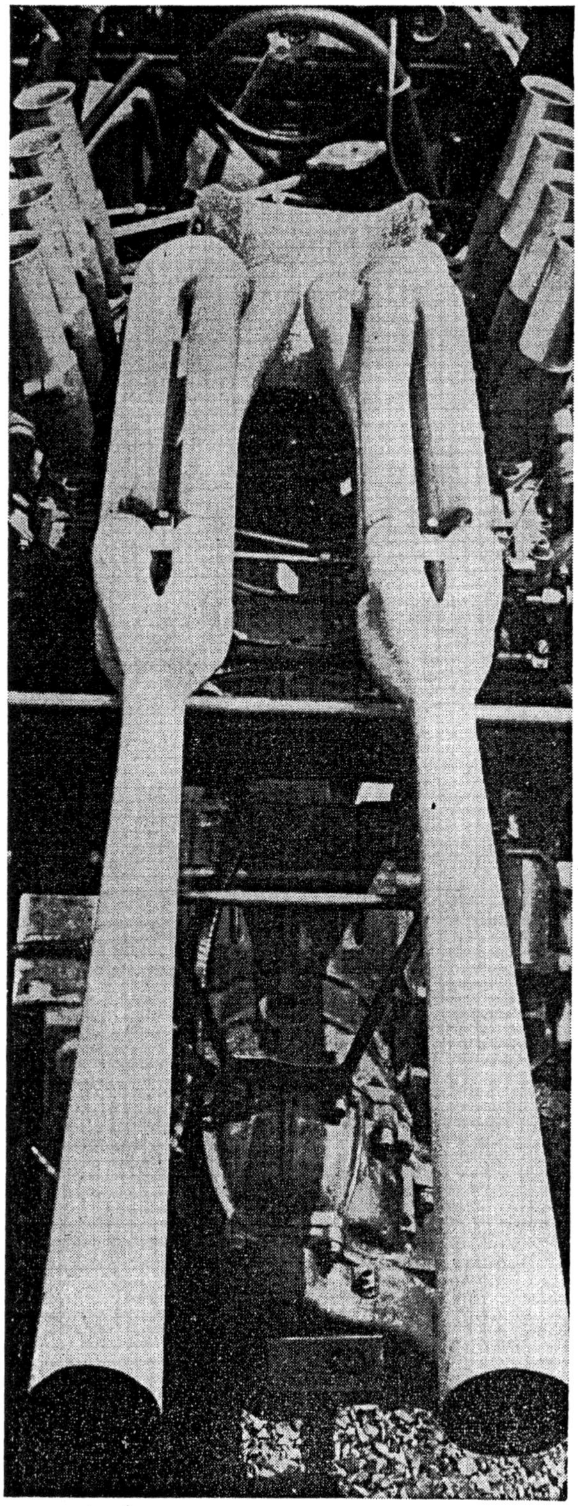

## Repco is going to prove Jack's win was no fluke.

**THE engine which Jack Brabham will be using in the Tasman series and in the early world championship races overseas is lighter and more powerful than the engine he had last year.**

Repco's racing engine chief, Frank Hallam, is not too keen at the moment about releasing hard facts on what changes have been made to the new engine or about what Jack will have pushing him along towards the end of this season.

But it will certainly be competitive with anything any other driver will have.

Repco has seen Jack's win last year give it a big boost in world markets, and its engineers are doing everything they can to make sure that last year's victory doesn't look like beginner's luck.

The new engine is giving 20 to 30 more brake horsepower than last year, according to sources inside the Repco organisation and, when it wears the new Repco block, will be some 30lb. lighter than last year. The 3-litre Formula 1 engine is expected to deliver 350 reliable horsepower.

The lighter weight will mean that Jack's new Formula 1 cars will be almost right on the minimum weight allowed for a Grand Prix car, while his opposition will still be way overweight.

The extra power, allied to the Brabham car's superb roadholding, will be ample to push the car along as fast as its opposition. The new engine still has the previous engine's low fuel consumption, which will enable Brabham to save weight and get better aerodynamic efficiency, because he'll need less space for fuel.

From the outside the main changes to the engine are the relocated exhaust pipes, which now sprout from between the camshaft covers instead of beneath them, and an altered timing case cover. The changes have permitted Repco to run vertical valves instead of the previous model's inclined ones and this, in turn, has permitted a better-shaped combustion chamber and more effective manifolding.

The changes to the head meant the camshafts had to be relocated and the engineers took the opportunity to add an extra sprocket and give more chain "wraparound" to the distributor drive to ensure greater reliability.

Although the 2.5-litre engines will use the same imported blocks as last year's engines, the 3-litre engines will have a locally made block with "wet" cylinder liners. This will solve the problem of uneven cylinder bore wear, which was inclined to cause heavy oil consumption in last year's engines.

We believe Repco will build an entirely new V8 for Jack to use towards the end of this year if he finds his opposition hard to toss. The new engine will be more complicated than the current version and will probably incorporate twin overhead camshafts.

The new Repco-Brabham as it appeared at the New Zealand Grand Prix. Silver material beneath the exhaust pipes keeps radiated heat from affecting the fuel injection equipment.

# Win for Brabham in Sandown International

*The Cooper trio of Brabham, Surtees and McLaren along one of the straights during the final of the Sandown International*

**AFTER holding a slender lead for most of the 120-mile international race on the new Sandown Park circuit near Melbourne, Jack Brabham took the chequered flag for his first major win in Australasia this season. Just 0·8sec away in second place was John Surtees in the Bowmaker-Yeoman 2·7 Cooper. Chuck Daigh, who put up an impressive performance with the new rear-engined Scarab, beat Stirling Moss in the 2·7 Lotus to fourth place.**

Team Lotus had provided last year's well-used works car for Jimmy Clark and a 2·5 Climax had replaced the 1,500 c.c. unit for this *formule libre* race. Lance Reventlow's new rear-engined Scarab was powered by a 3·9-litre vee-8 Buick breathing through four Weber carburettors and driving through a Cooper five-speed box.

### Sorting Out

Practice was on Friday and Saturday with two qualifying heats on Sunday and the main event on Monday. Friday's effort was only a try-out for the cars and times did not mean too much as gear ratios and carburation were sorted out. A torrential downpour which later flooded the pits did not help matters. On Saturday morning, Moss tried the Cooper, but decided to use the Lotus.

Daigh was pedalling the Scarab around fast enough to worry the other drivers and managed to stay with McLaren's 2·7 Cooper for a few laps. The Scarab would blast away from the Cooper out of corners, but the Cooper had the advantage on braking and in actual cornering. Fastest practice time for Saturday went to Brabham at 1min 8·1sec, with Surtees not far behind at 1min 8·9sec. Then came McLaren and Moss with 1min 9·4sec each. Moss had called at the pits every few laps to have another burst of fire extinguisher fluid in the clutch which was slipping badly.

Two 15-lap (30-mile) race heats were scheduled for Sunday, and, in the first one, Brabham, Surtees, McLaren and Daigh were drawn. Brabham jumped away to a good start with Surtees on his tail and McLaren battling hard to get past the Scarab. He got by on lap 3 and began closing on Brabham and Surtees. By lap 7 the three cars were nose to tail, but on the next lap Brabham pointed to his fuel tank and came past the pits the next time in third place with Surtees in the lead. Brabham's fuel pressure had dropped and so did his race position, although he managed to finish 20·5sec ahead of the Scarab.

Moss was the favourite for the second heat with no real opposition although Australian driver Bib Stillwell drove his 2·5 Cooper in an impressive fashion to stick with him and finish 1·5sec behind. Stillwell had been over-anxious on the starting line and had been penalized a minute for jumping the start, which dropped him to fifth place and elevated Jimmy Clark to second.

With a lap to go in his heat, Stirling entered the "S"-bend at around 100 m.p.h. and found a Cooper in his path. The startled driver braked and Stirling ran the nose of the Lotus under his tail. The Lotus went sideways and came out of what could have been a nasty incident with only damaged bodywork.

The Monday race day dawned fine and warm, and after a series of minor races the grid formed up for the 120-mile Sandown International Cup. Positions were taken from heat times, and Surtees was on pole with 17min 41·9sec, a time equalled by McLaren although Surtees beat him by a length; and filling the front row was Brabham who had bettered Moss' heat time by 3sec despite his fuel troubles. Stirling was beside the Scarab on the second row.

Brabham was first past the pits with McLaren hot on his tail. A break then to Surtees who was coming up fast and leading Daigh in the Scarab, Stillwell, Clark in the works Lotus, Moss, and Patterson in his 2·5 Cooper. By lap three Surtees had closed up on McLaren and Brabham, and on this lap Stillwell went out with a rod through the side of his motor.

One second covered the first three cars and they had already drawn out a 10sec gap over the Scarab. Surtees was pressing hard and he went by McLaren on lap 7, and took over the lead from Brabham five laps later.

A battle royal was being waged for fourth and fifth between Daigh in the Scarab and Moss in the Lotus, and it appeared as though Daigh had the upper hand—in power at least. The Buick vee-8 would rocket away from the Lotus coming out of corners, and although Stirling usually out-braked and out-cornered the American he just could not live with him on the straight.

On lap 22 Brabham took over his lead again, and the order of the first three stayed the same for the rest of the race. While lapping a particularly large number of stragglers, McLaren was left behind a few seconds, but he soon made the deficit up although he could make no impression on Surtees.

### Moss Is Lapped

On lap 50 Brabham brought his trio in behind the Scarab-Lotus duel, watched for a couple of laps, and then the three cars were by and Moss was lapped.

Brabham, Surtees and McLaren seemed to be satisfied with their positions in the final laps, but Stirling was pulling all the stops out in an effort to get by the Scarab. On each straight Daigh would leave him behind under acceleration.

And so the race ended with Brabham having a well-earned home win, 0·8sec ahead of John Surtees who had won the Longford race in Tasmania the previous weekend. Third, 3·2sec behind, was Bruce McLaren who had the lap record of 1min 8·7sec (104·8 m.p.h.) to his credit during the chase, and fourth, a lap behind, was Daigh in the new Scarab who led Moss across the line by a car's length.

**60 laps**

1, Cooper (J. Brabham), 1hour 10min 8·6sec; 2, Cooper (J. Surtees), 1hour 10min 9·4sec; 3, Cooper (B. McLaren), 1hour 10min 12·6sec; 4, Scarab (C. Daigh), 1hour 10min 20sec, 59 laps; 5, Lotus (S. Moss), 1hour 10min 20·3sec, 59 laps; 6, Lotus (J. Clark), 58 laps; 7, Cooper (B. Patterson), 57 laps; 8, Aston Martin (L. Davison), 57 laps.

When Cooper no longer built a competitive car for Jack Brabham, he manufactured his own

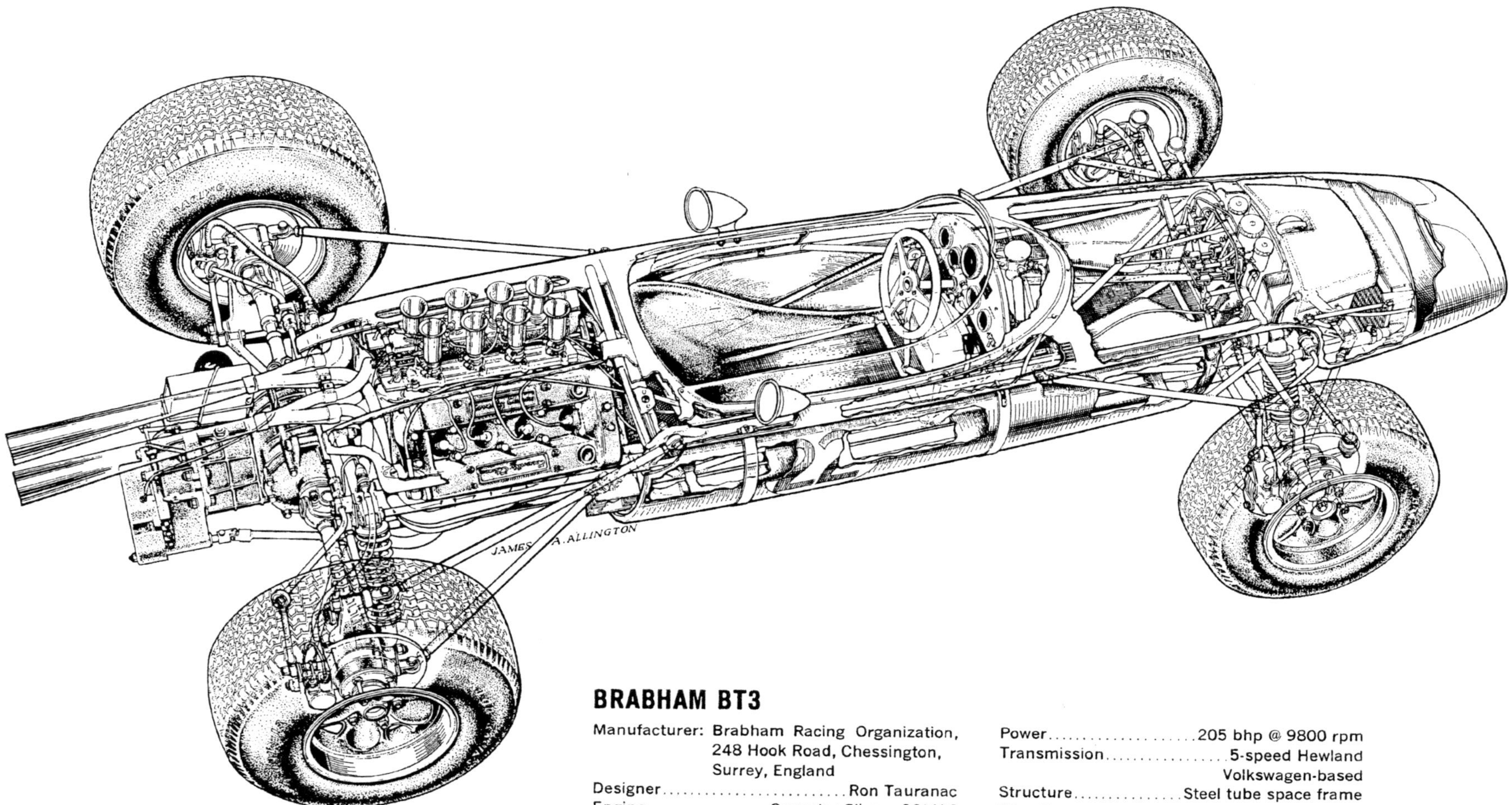


**BRABHAM BT3**

| | |
|---|---|
| Manufacturer: | Brabham Racing Organization, 248 Hook Road, Chessington, Surrey, England |
| Designer | Ron Tauranac |
| Engine | Coventry Climax 90° V-8 |
| Bore x stroke | 68 x 51.5 mm |
| Stroke/bore ratio | 0.76 to one |
| Displacement | 1496 cc |
| Compression ratio | 11.5 to one |
| Carburetion | Lucas fuel injection |
| Ignition | Lucas electronic |
| Power | 205 bhp @ 9800 rpm |
| Transmission | 5-speed Hewland Volkswagen-based |
| Structure | Steel tube space frame |
| Wheelbase | 91 in |
| Track | F 56 in, R 56 in |
| Length | 153 in |
| Body width | 36 in |
| Height | 29.5 in |
| Frontal area | 4.7 sq ft |
| Weight | 1020 lbs |

The Brabham Organization has created a good impression in its first full season of motor racing, and has really deserved better results than it has so far achieved; if there is such a thing as bad luck in motor racing then Jack Brabham and Dan Gurney have had far more than their fair share of it. It all started at Monaco, where both had engines fitted with a special new type of valve—and both had valves break in practice. Brabham flew his engine back to England, had it repaired and brought it back to be refitted in Gurney's car, only for Dan to have the ring and pinion break. At Spa Brabham was afflicted by electrical trouble, but Gurney was second in practice and third in the race.

At Zandvoort Gurney's engine seized, so he had no practice other than a few laps in Brabham's car. He went through the field from last place to fourth, but then had to make a pit-stop to have a loose fuel line secured; in spite of this he subsequently worked his way up to second place. Brabham had held second place early in the race until a throttle spring broke.

Low exhaust-pipe version of the Brabham is later version than that shown in cutaway.

At Reims both cars had fuel starvation trouble in practice, which was overcome by removing the fuel filters. In the race Gurney was lying second when his gear lever broke off, and Brabham later lost an almost certain second place when an electrical lead came loose. At Silverstone Brabham and Gurney were first and second for the first few glorious laps, but both subsequently had their engines blow for no apparent reason; Gurney was in second place at the time.

Brabham won the non-Championship Solitude race, but the German Grand Prix was a complete fiasco for the team, for Gurney's car suffered from fuel starvation throughout both practice and the race, and Jack's electronic ignition system packed up on the line, with the result that he started half a lap in arrears.

And so to Monza, where Gurney had his best race of the year, dueling for the lead with Clark until the 63rd lap—when the mysterious fuel starvation set in again. Brabham, too, had fuel feed trouble towards the end of the race, but only because the top tank would not drain; he eventually finished fifth. Strangely, Gurney's fuel system, with two pumps, is exactly the same as on Brabham's car, which has never had this trouble.

The Brabham is a very straightforward design, with an "old-fashioned" multi-tubular chassis, but suspension refinements have made it one of the best handling cars on the circuits.

Brabham suspension is based on roll centers which are relatively high by Formula One standards at 4 inches front, 4½ inches rear; by comparison the Lotus roll centers are 1 inch front, 1½ inches rear. At the front the wheels are located by extremely widebased wishbones—one leading, one trailing—and twin transverse links and double radius arms are used at the rear. The coil spring/damper units are conventionally mounted in each case. During the season the layout of the front suspension has been altered slightly to reduce nose dive under braking, the latter promoting excessive negative camber and thereby reducing the amount of rubber on the road. Thirteen-inch wheels, with 5.50 tires on 6-inch rims, are used at the front, while the rear wheels are 15 inch, with 6.50 tires on 7-inch rims.

The chassis is a well-triangulated space frame made up of small diameter, thin gauge (mostly 1 inch and ¾ inch, 18 gauge) mild steel tubing. The engine is rigidly mounted and effectively increases the car's overall stiffness. Transmission is by a Brabham-modified 5-speed Hewland-VW gearbox, and the drive shafts incorporate sliding splines, due to the difficulty of accommodating low friction pot joints (which have been used on a number of occasions) or rubber couplings.

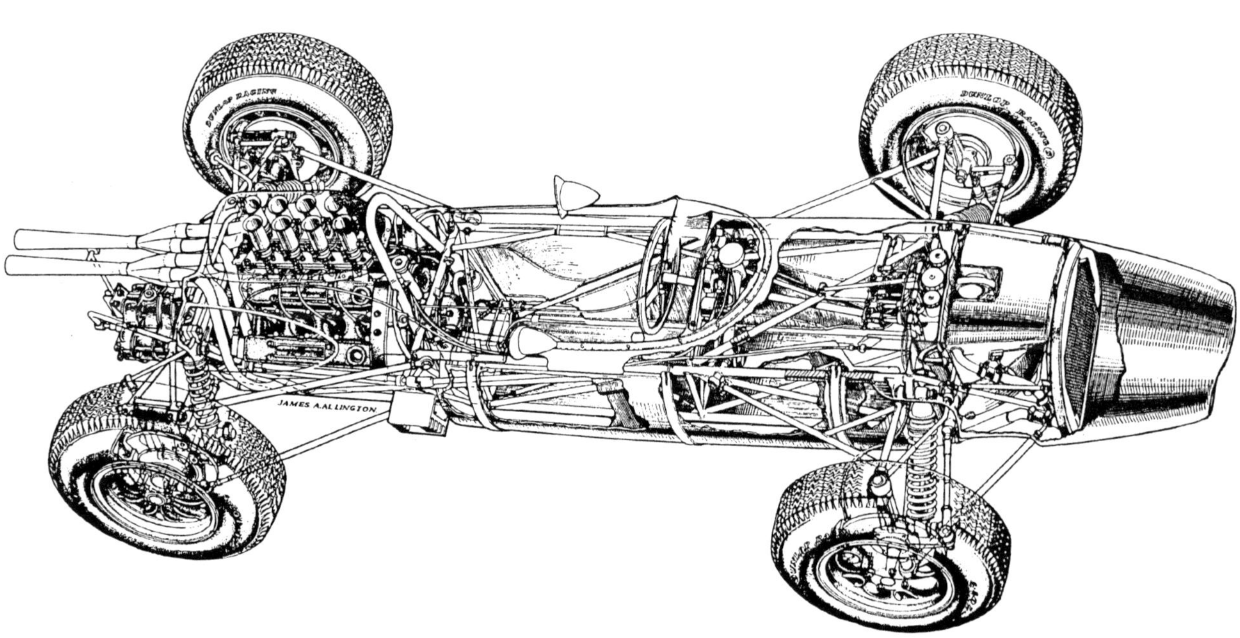

# BRABHAM - RESULTS FOR BRABHAM RACING ORGANISATION LTD

| DATE | EVENT | DRIVER | CAR | NO. | RESULT |
|---|---|---|---|---|---|
| 2 January 1967 | South African Grand Prix | D. Hulme | REPco V8 | 2 | 4th Place |
| 2 January 1967 | South African Grand Prix | J. Brabham | REPco V8 | 1 | 6th Place |
| 7 May 1967 | Monaco Grand Prix | D. Hulme | REPcoV8 | 9 | 1st Place (time of 2h34' 34.3") |
| 7 May 1967 | Monaco Grand Prix | J. Brabham | REPco V8 | 8 | Retired |
| 4 June 1967 | Dutch Grand Prix | J. Brabham | REPco V8 | 1 | 2nd Place (time of 2h 15' 08.7") |
| 4 June 1967 | Dutch Grand Prix | D. Hulme | REPco V8 | 2 | 3rd Place (time of 2h 15' 10.8") |
| 18 June 1967 | Belgian Grand Prix | J. Brabham | REPco V8 | 25 | Retired |
| 18 June 1967 | Belgian Grand Prix | D. Hulme | REPco V8 | 26 | Retired |
| 2 July 1967 | French Grand Prix | J. Brabham | REPco V8 | 3 | 1st Place (time of 2h 13' 21.3") |
| 2 July 1967 | French Grand Prix | D. Hulme | REPco V8 | 4 | 2nd Place (time of 2h 14' 10.8") |
| 15 July 1967 | British Grand Prix | D. Hulme | REPco V8 | 2 | 2nd Place (time of 1h 59' 38.4") |
| 15 July 1967 | British Grand Prix | J. Brabham | REPco V8 | 1 | 4th Place (time of 1h 59' 47.4") |
| 6 August 1967 | German Grand Prix | D. Hulme | REPco V8 | 2 | 1st Place (winning time of 2h 05' 55.7") |
| 6 August 1967 | German Grand Prix | J. Brabham | REPco V8 | 2 | 2nd Place (time of 2h 06' 34.2") |
| 27 August 1967 | Canadian Grand Prix | J. Brabham | REPco V8 | 1 | 1st Place (winning time of 2h 40' 00.0" |
| 27 August 1967 | Canadian Grand Prix | D. Hulme | REPco V8 | 2 | 2nd Place (time of 2h 41' 09.0" |

# BRABHAM - RESULTS FOR BRABHAM RACING ORGANISATION LTD

| DATE | EVENT | DRIVER | CAR | NO. | RESULT |
|---|---|---|---|---|---|
| 10 September 1967 | Italian Grand Prix | J. Brabham | REPco V8 | 16 | 2nd Place (time of 1h 43' 45.2") |
| 10 September 1967 | Italian Grand Prix | D. Hulme | REPco V8 | 18 | Retired |
| 1 October 1967 | United States Grand Prix | J. Brabham | REPco V8 | 1 | 5th Place (time of 2h 3' 41.0") |
| 1 October 1967 | United States Grand Prix | D. Hulme | REPco V8 | 2 | 3rd Place (time of 2h 4' 01.0") |
| 22 October 1967 | Mexican Grand Prix | J. Brabham | REPco V8 | 1 | 2nd Place (time of 2h 00' 54.06") |
| 22 October 1967 | Mexican Grand Prix | D. Hulme | REPco V8 | 2 | 3rd Place |
| 1 January 1968 | South African Grand Prix | J. Brabham | REPco V8 | 2 | Retired |
| 1 January 1968 | South African Grand Prix | J. Rindt | REPco V8 | 3 | 3rd Place (time of 1h 54' 27.0") |
| 12 May 1968 | Spanish Grand Prix | J. Rindt | REPco V8 | 4 | Retired |
| 26 May 1968 | Monaco Grand Prix | J. Brabham | REPco V8 | 2 | Retired |
| 26 May 1968 | Monaco Grand Prix | J. Rindt | REPco V8 | 3 | Retired |
| 9 June 1968 | Belgian Grand Prix | J. Brabham | REPco V8 | 18 | Retired |
| 9 June 1968 | Belgian Grand Prix | J. Rindt | REPco V8 | 19 | Retired |
| 23 June 1968 | Dutch Grand Prix | J. Brabham | REPco V8 | 5 | Retired |
| 23 June 1968 | Dutch Grand Prix | J. Rindt | REPco V8 | 6 | Retired |
| 7 July 1968 | French Grand Prix | J. Rindt | REPco V8 | 2 | Retired |
| 7 July 1968 | French Grand Prix | J. Brabham | REPco V8 | 4 | Retired |

# BRABHAM - RESULTS FOR BRABHAM RACING ORGANISATION LTD

| DATE | EVENT | DRIVER | CAR | NO. | RESULT |
|---|---|---|---|---|---|
| 20 July 1968 | British Grand Prix | J. Brabham | REPco V8 | 3 | Retired |
| 20 July 1968 | British Grand Prix | J. Rindt | REPco V8 | 4 | Retired |
| 4 August 1968 | German Grand Prix | J. Brabham | REPco V8 | 4 | 5th Place (time of 2h 25' 24.3") |
| 4 August 1968 | German Grand Prix | J. Rindt | REPco V8 | 5 | 3rd Place (time of 2h 23' 12.6") |
| 8 September 1968 | Italian Grand Prix | J. Brabham | REPco V8 | 10 | Retired |
| 8 September 1968 | Italian Grand Prix | J. Rindt | REPco V8 | 11 | Retired |
| 22 September 1968 | Canadian Grand Prix | J. Brabham | REPco V8 | 5 | Retired |
| 22 September 1968 | Canadian Grand Prix | J. Rindt | REPco V8 | 6 | Retired |
| 6 October 1968 | United States Grand Prix | J. Brabham | REPco V8 | 3 | Retired |
| 6 October 1968 | United States Grand Prix | J. Rindt | REPco V8 | 4 | Retired |
| 3 November 1968 | Mexican Grand Prix | J. Brabham | REPco V8 | 3 | 10th Place |
| 3 November 1968 | Mexican Grand Prix | J. Rindt | REPco V8 | 4 | Retired |
| 1 March 1969 | South African Grand Prix | J. Brabham | BT26 | 14 | Retired |
| 1 March 1969 | South African Grand Prix | J. Ickx | BT26 | 15 | Retired |
| 4 May 1969 | Spanish Grand Prix | J. Brabham | BT26 | 3 | Retired |
| 4 May 1969 | Spanish Grand Prix | J. Ickx | BT26 | 4 | 6th Place |
| 8 June 1969 | Monaco Grand Prix | J. Brabham | BT26 | 5 | Retired |

# BRABHAM - RESULTS FOR BRABHAM RACING ORGANISATION LTD

| DATE | EVENT | DRIVER | CAR | NO. | RESULT |
|---|---|---|---|---|---|
| 8 June 1969 | Monaco Grand Prix | J. Ickx | BT26 | 6 | Retired |
| 21 June 1969 | Dutch Grand Prix | J. Brabham | BT26 | 11 | 6$^{th}$ Place (time of 2h 07' 52.89") |
| 21 June 1969 | Dutch Grand Prix | J. Ickx | BT26 | 12 | 5$^{th}$ Place (time of 2h 07' 19.75") |
| 6 July 1969 | French Grand Prix | J. Ickx | BT26 | 11 | 3$^{rd}$ Place (time of 1h 57' 44.7") |
| 19 July 1969 | British Grand Prix | J. Ickx | BT26 | 7 | 2$^{nd}$ Place (time of 1h 56' 36.1") |
| 3 August 1969 | German Grand Prix | J. Ickx | BT26 | 6 | 1$^{st}$ Place (winning time of 1h 49' 55.4) |
| 8 September 1969 | Italian Grand Prix | J. Brabham | BT26 | 28 | Retired |
| 8 September 1969 | Italian Grand Prix | J. Ickx | BT26 | 26 | 10$^{th}$ Place |
| 20 September 1969 | Canadian Grand Prix | J. Brabham | BT26 | 12 | 2$^{nd}$ Place (time of 2h 00' 11.9") |
| 20 September 1969 | Canadian Grand Prix | J. Ickx | BT26 | 11 | 1$^{st}$ Place (winning time of 1h 59' 25.7") |
| 5 October 1969 | United States Grand Prix | J. Ickx | BT26 | 7 | Retired |
| 5 October 1969 | United States Grand Prix | J. Brabham | BT26 | 8 | 4$^{th}$ Place (time of 1h 59' 2.38") |
| 19 October 1969 | Mexican Grand Prix | J. Ickx | BT26 | 7 | 2$^{nd}$ Place (time of 1h 54' 11.36") |
| 19 October 1969 | Mexican Grand Prix | J. Brabham | BT26 | 8 | 3$^{rd}$ Place (time of 1h 54' 47.28") |
| 7 March 1970 | South African Grand Prix | J. Brabham | BT33 | 12 | 1$^{st}$ Place (winning time of 1h 49' 34.6") |
| 19 April | Spanish Grand Prix | J. Brabham | BT33 | 7 | Retired |

# BRABHAM - RESULTS FOR BRABHAM RACING ORGANISATION LTD

| DATE | EVENT | DRIVER | CAR | NO. | RESULT |
|---|---|---|---|---|---|
| 10 May 1970 | Monaco Grand Prix | J. Brabham | BT33 | 5 | 2nd Place (time of 1h 54' 59.7") |
| 7 June 1970 | Belgian Grand Prix | J. Brabham | BT33 | 18 | Retired |
| 21 June 1970 | Dutch Grand Prix | J. Brabham | BT33 | 18 | 11th Place |
| 5 July 1970 | French Grand Prix | J. Brabham | BT33 | 23 | 3rd Place (time of 1h 56' 41.83") |
| 18 July 1970 | British Grand Prix | J. Brabham | BT33 | 17 | 2nd Place (time of 1h 57' 34.9") |
| 2 August 1970 | German Grand Prix | J. Brabham | BT33 | 3 | Retired |
| 16 August 1970 | Austrian Grand Prix | J. Brabham | BT33 | 10 | 13th Place |
| 8 September 1970 | Italian Grand Prix | J. Brabham | BT33 | 44 | Retired |
| 20 September 1970 | Canadian Grand Prix | J. Brabham | BT33 | 11 | Retired |
| 4 October 1970 | United States Grand Prix | J. Brabham | BT33 | 15 | 10th Place |
| 18 October 1970 | Mexican Grand Prix | J. Brabham | BT33 | 15 | Retired |
| 6 March 1971 | South African Grand Prix | G. Hill | BT33 | - | - |
| 6 March 1971 | South African Grand Prix | D. Charlton | BT33 | 15 | Retired |
| 18 April 1971 | Spanish Grand Prix | G. Hill | BT34 | 7 | Retired |
| 18 April 1971 | Spanish Grand Prix | T. Schenken | BT33 | 8 | 9th Place |
| 23 May 1971 | Monaco Grand Prix | G. Hill | BT34 | 7 | Retired |
| 23 May 1971 | Monaco Grand Prix | T. Schenken | BT33 | 8 | 10th Place |

# BRABHAM - RESULTS FOR BRABHAM RACING ORGANISATION LTD

| DATE | EVENT | DRIVER | CAR | NO. | RESULT |
|---|---|---|---|---|---|
| 20 June 1971 | Dutch Grand Prix | G. Hill | BT34 | 24 | 10th Place |
| 20 June 1971 | Dutch Grand Prix | T. Schenken | BT34 | 25 | Retired |
| 4 July 1971 | French Grand Prix | G. Hill | BT34 | 7 | Retired |
| 4 July 1971 | French Grand Prix | T. Schenken | BT33 | 8 | Retired |
| 17 July 1971 | British Grand Prix | G. Hill | BT34 | 7 | Retired |
| 17 July 1971 | British Grand Prix | T. Schenken | BT33 | 8 | Retired |
| 1 August 1971 | German Grand Prix | G. Hill | BT34 | 24 | 9th Place |
| 1 August 1971 | German Grand Prix | T. Schenken | BT33 | 25 | 6th Place (time of 1h 32' 14.3") |
| 15 August 1971 | Austrian Grand Prix | G. Hill | BT34 | 7 | 5th Place (time of 1h 31' 12.34") |
| 15 August 1971 | Austrian Grand Prix | T. Schenken | BT33 | 8 | 3rd Place (time of 1h 30' 43.68") |
| 5 September 1971 | Italian Grand Prix | G. Hill | BT34 | 10 | Retired |
| 5 September 1971 | Italian Grand Prix | T. Schenken | BT33 | 11 | Retired |
| 19 September 1971 | Canadian Grand Prix | T. Schenken | BT33 | 8 | Retired |
| 19 September 1971 | Canadian Grand Prix | G. Hill | BT34 | 37 | Retired |
| 3 October 1971 | United States Grand Prix | G. Hill | BT34 | 22 | 7th Place |
| 3 October 1971 | United States Grand Prix | T. Schenken | BT33 | 23 | Retired |
| 3 October 1971 | United States Grand Prix | C. Craft | BT33 | 24 | Retired |

# BRABHAM - RESULTS FOR BRABHAM RACING ORGANISATION LTD

| DATE | EVENT | DRIVER | CAR | NO. | RESULT |
|---|---|---|---|---|---|
| 23 January 1972 | Argentine Grand Prix | G. Hill | BT33 | 1 | Retired |
| 23 January 1972 | Argentine Grand Prix | C. Reutemann | BT34 | 2 | 7th Place (time of 1h 57' 59.3") |
| 4 March 1972 | South African Grand Prix | G. Hill | BT33 | 19 | 6th Place (time of 1h 45' 54.5") |
| 4 March 1972 | South African Grand Prix | C. Reutemann | BT34 | 20 | Retired |
| 1 May 1972 | Spanish Grand Prix | G. Hill | BT37 | 18 | 10th Place (time of 2h 4' 6.92") |
| 1 May 1972 | Spanish Grand Prix | W. Fittipaldi | BT33 | 22 | 7th Place (time of 2h 4' 14.36") |
| 14 May 1972 | Monaco Grand Prix | G. Hill | BT37 | 20 | 12th Place |
| 14 May 1972 | Monaco Grand Prix | W. Fittipaldi | BT33 | 21 | 9th Place |
| 4 June 1972 | Belgian Grand Prix | G. Hill | BT37 | 17 | Retired |
| 4 June 1972 | Belgian Grand Prix | W. Fittipaldi | BT34 | 18 | Retired |
| 4 June 1972 | Belgian Grand Prix | C. Reutemann | BT37 | 19 | 13th Place |
| 4 July 1972 | French Grand Prix | G. Hill | BT37 | 18 | 10th Place (time of 1h 55' 21.0") |
| 4 July 1972 | French Grand Prix | W. Fittipaldi | BT34 | 19 | 8th Place (time of 1h 54' 46.6") |
| 4 July 1972 | French Grand Prix | C. Reutemann | BT37 | 20 | 12th Place |
| 17 July 1972 | European Grand Prix | G. Hill | BT37 | 26 | Retired |
| 17 July 1972 | European Grand Prix | C. Reutemann | BT37 | 27 | 8th Place (time of 1h 48' 30.1") |
| 17 July 1972 | European Grand Prix | W. Fittipaldi | BT34 | 28 | 12th Place |

# BRABHAM - RESULTS FOR BRABHAM RACING ORGANISATION LTD

| DATE | EVENT | DRIVER | CAR | NO. | RESULT |
|---|---|---|---|---|---|
| 1 August 1972 | German Grand Prix | G. Hill | BT37 | 11 | 6$^{th}$ Place (time of 1h 45' 11.9") |
| 1 August 1972 | German Grand Prix | C. Reutemann | BT37 | 12 | Retired |
| 1 August 1972 | German Grand Prix | W. Fittipaldi | BT34 | 26 | 7$^{th}$ Place (time of 1h 45' 12.4") |
| 13 August 1972 | Austrian Grand Prix | G. Hill | BT37 | 16 | Retired |
| 13 August 1972 | Austrian Grand Prix | C. Reutemann | BT37 | 17 | Retired |
| 13 August 1972 | Austrian Grand Prix | W. Fittipaldi | BT34 | 28 | Retired |
| 10 September 1972 | Italian Grand Prix | G. Hill | BT37 | 28 | 5$^{th}$ Place (time of 1h 31' 4.0") |
| 10 September 1972 | Italian Grand Prix | W. Fittipaldi | BT34 | 29 | Retired |
| 10 September 1972 | Italian Grand Prix | C. Reutemann | BT37 | 30 | Retired |
| 24 September 1972 | Canadian Grand Prix | G. Hill | BT37 | 7 | 8$^{th}$ Place |
| 24 September 1972 | Canadian Grand Prix | C. Reutemann | BT37 | 8 | 4$^{th}$ Place (time of 1h 44' 17.6") |
| 24 September 1972 | Canadian Grand Prix | W. Fittipaldi | BT34 | 9 | Retired |
| 8 October 1972 | United States Grand Prix | G. Hill | BT37 | 28 | 11$^{th}$ Place |
| 8 October 1972 | United States Grand Prix | C. Reutemann | BT37 | 29 | Retired |
| 28 January 1973 | Argentine Grand Prix | C. Reutemann | BT37 | 10 | Retired |
| 28 January 1973 | Argentine Grand Prix | W. Fittipaldi | BT37 | 12 | 6$^{th}$ Place |
| 11 February 1973 | Brazilian Grand Prix | C. Reutemann | BT37 | 17 | 11$^{th}$ Place |

# BRABHAM - RESULTS FOR BRABHAM RACING ORGANISATION LTD

| DATE | EVENT | DRIVER | CAR | NO. | RESULT |
|---|---|---|---|---|---|
| 11 February 1973 | Brazilian Grand Prix | W. Fittipaldi | BT37 | 18 | Retired |
| 3 March 1973 | South African Grand Prix | C. Reutemann | BT37 | 18 | 7th Place |
| 3 March 1973 | South African Grand Prix | W. Fittipaldi | BT37 | 19 | Retired |
| 29 April 1973 | Spanish Grand Prix | W. Fittipaldi | BT42 | 17 | 10th Place |
| 29 April 1973 | Spanish Grand Prix | C. Reutemann | BT42 | 18 | Retired |
| 20 May 1973 | European Grand Prix | C. Reutemann | BT42 | 10 | Retired |
| 20 May 1973 | European Grand Prix | W. Fittipaldi | BT42 | 11 | Retired |
| 3 June 1973 | Monaco Grand Prix | C. Reutemann | BT42 | 10 | Retired |
| 3 June 1973 | Monaco Grand Prix | W. Fittipaldi | BT42 | 11 | Retired |
| 17 June 1973 | Swedish Grand Prix | C. Reutemann | BT42 | 10 | 4th Place (time of 1h 57' 4.12") |
| 17 June 1973 | Swedish Grand Prix | W. Fittipaldi | BT42 | 11 | Retired |
| 1 July 1973 | French Grand Prix | C. Reutemann | BT42 | 10 | 3rd Place (time of 1h 42' 23.0") |
| 1 July 1973 | French Grand Prix | W. Fittipaldi | BT42 | 11 | 16th Place |
| 14 July 1973 | British Grand Prix | C. Reutemann | BT42 | 10 | 6th Place (time of 1h 30' 3.2") |
| 14 July 1973 | British Grand Prix | W. Fittipaldi | BT42 | 11 | Retired |
| 29 July 1973 | Dutch Grand Prix | C. Reutemann | BT42 | 10 | Retired |
| 29 July 1973 | Dutch Grand Prix | W. Fittipaldi | BT42 | 11 | Retired |

# BRABHAM - RESULTS FOR BRABHAM RACING ORGANISATION LTD

| DATE | EVENT | DRIVER | CAR | NO. | RESULT |
|---|---|---|---|---|---|
| 5 August 1973 | German Grand Prix | C. Reutemann | BT42 | 10 | Retired |
| 5 August 1973 | German Grand Prix | W. Fittipaldi | BT42 | 11 | 5th Place (time of 1h 43' 22.9") |
| 19 August 1973 | Austrian Grand Prix | R. Stommelen | BT42 | 9 | Retired |
| 19 August 1973 | Austrian Grand Prix | C. Reutemann | BT42 | 10 | 4th Place (time of 1h 29' 36.69") |
| 19 August 1973 | Austrian Grand Prix | W. Fittipaldi | BT42 | 11 | Retired |
| 9 September 1973 | Italian Grand Prix | R. Stommelen | BT42 | 9 | 12th Place |
| 9 September 1973 | Italian Grand Prix | C. Reutemann | BT42 | 10 | 6th Place (time of 1h 30' 16.8") |
| 9 September 1973 | Italian Grand Prix | W. Fittipaldi | BT42 | 11 | Retired |
| 23 September 1973 | Canadian Grand Prix | R. Stommelen | BT42 | 9 | 12th Place |
| 23 September 1973 | Canadian Grand Prix | C. Reutemann | BT42 | 10 | 8th Place |
| 23 September 1973 | Canadian Grand Prix | W. Fittipaldi | BT42 | 11 | 11th Place |
| 7 October 1973 | United States Grand Prix | J. Watson | BT42 | 9 | Retired |
| 7 October 1973 | United States Grand Prix | C. Reutemann | BT42 | 10 | 3rd Place (time of 1h 41' 38.72") |
| 7 October 1973 | United States Grand Prix | W. Fittipaldi | | 11 | Running, not classified |
| 13 January 1974 | Argentine Grand Prix | C. Reutemann | | 7 | 7th Place |
| 13 January 1974 | Argentine Grand Prix | R. Robarts | | 8 | Retired |
| 27 January 1974 | Brazilian Grand Prix | C. Reutemann | | 7 | 7th Place (time of 1h 23' 9.55") |

# BRABHAM - RESULTS FOR BRABHAM RACING ORGANISATION LTD

| DATE | EVENT | DRIVER | CAR | NO. | RESULT |
|---|---|---|---|---|---|
| 27 January 1974 | Brazilian Grand Prix | R. Robarts | | 8 | 15th Place |
| 30th March 1974 | South African Grand Prix | C. Reutemann | | 7 | 1st Place (winning time of 1h 42' 40.96") |
| 30th March 1974 | South African Grand Prix | R. Robarts | | 8 | 17th Place |
| 28 April 1974 | Spanish Grand Prix | C. Reutemann | | 7 | Retired |
| 28 April 1974 | Spanish Grand Prix | R. von Opel | | 8 | Retired |
| 17 May 1974 | Belgian Grand Prix | C. Reutemann | | 7 | Retired |
| 17 May 1974 | Belgian Grand Prix | R. von Opel | | 8 | Retired |
| 26 May 1974 | Monaco Grand Prix | C. Reutemann | BT44 | 7 | Retired |
| 9 June 1974 | Swedish Grand Prix | C. Reutemann | BT44 | 7 | Retired |
| 9 June 1974 | Swedish Grand Prix | R. von Opel | BT44 | 8 | 9th Place |
| 23 June 1974 | Dutch Grand Prix | C. Reutemann | BT44 | 7 | 12th Place |
| 23 June 1974 | Dutch Grand Prix | R. von Opel | BT44 | 8 | 9th Place |
| 7 July 1974 | French Grand Prix | C. Reutemann | BT44 | 7 | Retired |
| 20 July 1974 | British Grand Prix | C. Pace | BT44 | 8 | 9th Place |
| 20 July 1974 | British Grand Prix | C. Reutemann | BT44 | 7 | 6th Place (time of 1h 43' 11.5") |
| 4 August 1974 | German Grand Prix | C. Reutemann | BT44 | 7 | 3rd Place (time of 1h 42' 58.2") |
| 4 August 1974 | German Grand Prix | C. Pace | BT44 | 8 | 12th Place |

# BRABHAM - RESULTS FOR BRABHAM RACING ORGANISATION LTD

| DATE | EVENT | DRIVER | CAR | NO. | RESULT |
|---|---|---|---|---|---|
| 18 August 1974 | Austrian Grand Prix | C. Reutemann | BT44 | 7 | 1st Place (winning time of 1h 28' 44.72") |
| 18 August 1974 | Austrian Grand Prix | C. Pace | BT44 | 8 | Retired |
| 8 September 1974 | Italian Grand Prix | C. Reutemann | BT44 | 7 | Retired |
| 8 September 1974 | Italian Grand Prix | C. Pace | BT44 | 8 | 5th Place (time of 1h 23' 0.2") |
| 22 September 1974 | Canadian Grand Prix | C. Reutemann | BT44 | 7 | 9th Place |
| 22 September 1974 | Canadian Grand Prix | C. Pace | BT44 | 8 | 8th Place |
| 6 October 1974 | United States Grand Prix | C. Reutemann | BT44 | 7 | 1st Place (winning time of 1h 40' 21.44") |
| 6 October 1974 | United States Grand Prix | C. Pace | BT44 | 8 | 2nd Place (time of 1h 40' 32.17") |

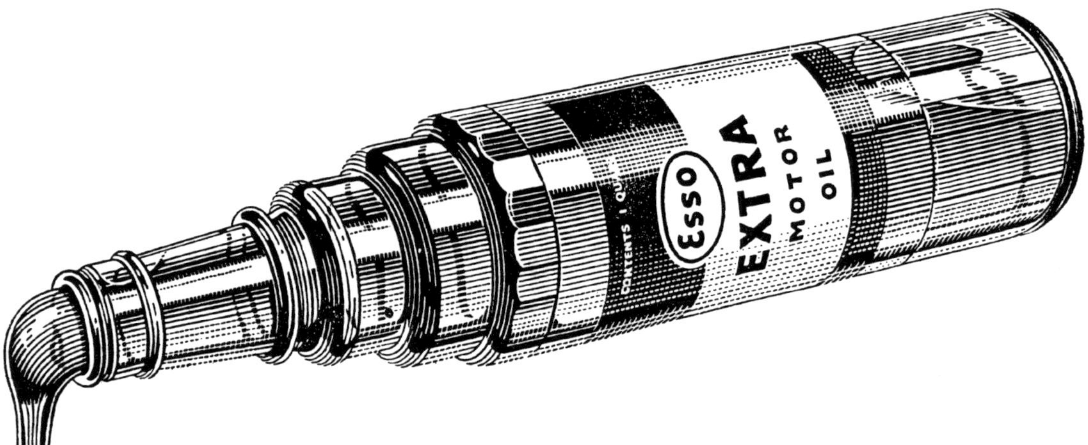
Esso
EXTRA
MOTOR
OIL

**TRACK TEST** No. 15

**by JOHN BLUNSDEN, the only journalist to have driven the Brabham-Ford—an outstanding new Junior which is providing valuable lessons for the eagerly awaited grand prix machine**

# THE BRABHAM JUNIOR

MY enthusiastic acceptance of Jack Brabham's offer to try his new Junior at Goodwood was tempered with a solemn thought; here was the perfect opportunity of proving just how slow I am!

Earlier in the day, Jack had spent quite a long time 'sorting' the car, and in the process had caused me to completely revise my evaluation of Formula Junior lap times at Goodwood. Under 1.40 I had thought reasonable for track-testing, under 1.35 distinctly promising for a race time, while 1.30 spelt something close to race-winning speed. How wrong I was!

Before Jack had pronounced the car 'right', he had lapped twice in 1 minute 26.8 seconds, and this despite someone else's sump full of oil which had been deposited neatly from one end of St. Mary's to the other. The track was so slippery there that it must have slowed the car by close on a second; so gentlemen, your bogy time is now 1.26. And the best of luck to you!

Any direct and odious comparison between the Brabham and Blunsden times was effectively foiled a few minutes before I climbed aboard by a deluge which, mixed with a high wind and the aforementioned oil, rendered the circuit something of a skating rink. But at least it simplified the task of finding out what happened when the wheels became unstuck!

First acquaintance with the Brabham brings an immediate respect for the quality of the workmanship which has gone into it. This seems to be a very robust Junior, built along fairly conventional lines, and finished to the standard that one might expect from the Brabham-Tauranac partnership.

## DIMPLES FOR STRENGTH

The main frame tubes are 1 inch 16 gauge round-section, and braced by ¾ inch 16 gauge round-section diagonals, except at the ends of the frame, where square and rectangular tubing is used for extra stiffness. There is a stressed cockpit panel of mild steel sheet, the main surfaces of which are dimpled for strength instead of being drilled.

The glass-fibre body is in three large sections, the centre moulding forming the floor of the car as well as the lower part of the body sides. Front and rear sections are quickly detachable in the usual way, and formed an easy and rigid fit. The car I tested, which is the works model to be driven by Frank Gardner, has an excellent finish and is sprayed in white with black wheels.

Front suspension is by compact wide-angle top wishbones and longer narrow-angle lower wishbones in conjunction with inclined coil springs and Armstrong GT7 dampers. A ½ inch anti-roll bar is also fitted at the front. The rear-end layout is a departure from normal practice in that the radius arms act as the leading members of the wishbones, the upper radius arm being linked to a single transverse strut, and the lower arm to the foremost of a pair of tubes linked at a single inboard pivot. Again, coil springs and Armstrong GT7 dampers are fitted, the dampers in this case being mounted upside-down to reduce the unsprung weight. For a similar reason the rear brakes, (Girling 9½ inch), are mounted inboard, although the 9 inch discs at the front are adjacent to the wheel hubs.

Quick-change calipers are fitted, on the leading side of the disc in each case, the rear calipers being attached to special side plates which have been made to carry the auxiliary races for the output shafts from the VW five-speed gearbox.

The engine is a Ford 105E Holbay 1,100 cc unit, quoted at 100 horsepower at 7,200 rpm. The first production cars are being fitted with the normal wet-sump equipment, but the works car has a special dry-sump arrangement incorporating dual scavenge pumps driven from the front end of the camshaft, the complete system having a capacity of 2 gallons. The clutch is a Haussermann diaphragm-type unit, giving a very light pedal action.

The Brabham has its own rack-and-pinion steering, and Ron Tauranac has designed neat and efficient magnesium wheels with four-stud fixing and ventilation holes for brake cooling (at the front).

Tauranac has spurned the use of the chassis tubes for oil and water delivery on the grounds that separate tubes, if there is room for them, do not transmit heat to the rest of the frame. Oil and water are pumped from the engine along tubes running close to the bottom and top left frame members, respectively, and return by two adjacent tubes running alongside the bottom right frame member, the upper part of the cockpit on this side being taken up by the gear linkage and change lever.

## PLENTY OF WORKING ROOM

There is not a lot of space between the steering column and the dry battery which rests behind the knees, so climbing in or out of the Brabham is something which calls for quite a technique. But although this is no car for a Le Mans start, (how about that for sorting out these Formula Junior starts?) once installed, the driver is given plenty of working room. The pedals are adjustable, and there is a foot rest to the left of the clutch.

The gear lever is conveniently sited just to the right of the steering wheel, and the instruments are easily read through the top segment of the wheel, these comprising an 8,000 rpm tachometer, flanked on the left by a water temperature gauge and on the right by a combined oil pressure and temperature gauge. This particular car was also equipped with a fuel pressure gauge on the extreme left.

When 'the boss' had been driving the car on the dry circuit it had been showing a tendency towards understeer, which had been partly cured by putting more air into the front tyres and taking some out of the rears. Jack had also given a lurid demonstration of the car's controllability when on one lap he braked for the chicane only to find that the car started to accelerate; the accelerator was wrongly adjusted and as he applied the brake the right pedal also went down. Realising he could not miss the wattle fencing Jack aimed the car between two pieces of fence, squeezed through, then put on sharp left lock on the grass to pull the car back on the course without hitting a thing!

Nosing the car away from the pits in something of a downpour, I pondered on what might happen if I tried a similar

**Above:** *The radiator and oil tank for the dry-sump Holbay-Ford engine are mounted on an extension of the main chassis frame. Water and oil are carried through their own plated and lagged mild steel tubes. The conventional double wishbone front suspension offers full adjustment for castor and camber.* **Below:** *The output of the engine fitted to the works car is 97 horsepower at 7,200 rpm, with a wide, usable rev range from 4,700 to 8,000 rpm.*

*Normal instrument layout includes a central rev counter, flanked by a combined oil pressure and temperature gauge, and a water temperature gauge. The works car also carries a fuel pressure gauge on the extreme left.*

## TRACK TEST | No. 15

manoeuvre on the soaking wet grass, also what excuse I should be able to offer, now that the accelerator had been readjusted. The answers being 'a lot' and 'none,' respectively, I applied what I took to be appropriate caution.

During a first careful lap sorting out the puddles, the oil, and the wind direction, I spent quite a lot of time playing with the gearbox, which without doubt I rate the best I have ever sampled on a Junior. The five speeds forward are laid out with the top four in the conventional 'H' and first right over to the left and back. There is also a reverse, immediately ahead of first. There was no catch protecting reverse on this car, (all production models will have one), so the lever had to be lifted gently out of first. A slight lip alongside second prevents the lever from moving right across the gate into fourth.

### STRAIGHT-THROUGH CHANGE

The action of the box is so light that there is an initial tendency to assume that the next gear has not been engaged, (on one occasion it wasn't!), and there is no question of double-declutching, for example, between fifth and fourth. The lever is simply slid straight forward in one clean movement, and the change is extremely rapid. Coupled with the light, smooth action of the diaphragm-type clutch, it makes gear-changing a most enjoyable business calling for the minimum of concentration. What a comforting feeling to know that should you have to grab another cog in a hurry, it will go in every time.

Settling down to the conditions I became bolder and found that the Holbay-Ford engine had an excellent range of useful power. The punch is first felt strongly at around 4,700 rpm, from which there is a progressive build-up to the peak output at 7,200 rpm, (this particular unit was giving 97 horsepower), with 8,000 rpm on tap should it be needed. I held this for a second or so in fourth gear to find the unit still as sweet as the proverbial nut. Some popping and banging occurs on the over-run from the middle of the rev range, but this did not seem to occur from the higher revs.

I make no pretence of having wrung the car's neck in these most unpleasant circuit conditions, but I noticed that on a stretch of Fordwater the effect of some surface ripples and irregular puddles was to induce a certain amount of 'shimmy' and lightness of control without affecting the general direction of travel. In this condition the car was virtually self-correcting, and when on one lap I found myself taking a wider line than I wanted for the final right-hand kink at Fordwater, I was able to tighten it up without any drama, the car really seeming to 'dig in' at this vital point.

The combination of changing torque on moving from fourth to fifth, changing road surface, and changing wind direction—all at the left-hand kink along the straight—caused the Brabham to move a foot or so to the right on every lap, but it was reassuring to find that the car immediately settled down again on a parallel line.

The ride is perhaps a little firmer than on some Juniors, without being 'choppy', and a mild amount of understeer was still evident when I tried the car; the high-sided seat held me firmly through the corners and the screen offers full protection round the shoulders.

For the conditions, the Brabham was over-braked, some lack of balance at the back being further inducement to tread lightly on the pedal. This was due to oil mist creeping on to one disc via the breather from an over-filled gearbox; the breather has since been modified to prevent a recurrence of the trouble in the event of the sump again being over-filled.

### LOST IT!

Already, the Brabham's calibre had been effectively demonstrated by Jack's sensational times on the dry circuit, and as I eased off along the straight before coming in I decided that Frank Gardner must be contemplating the season with some confidence. I was still thinking so as I rounded Woodcote, slower than before, and hit a puddle on the exit. In a flash the tail went to the left, and we executed a neat pirouette backwards on to the infield. Frank was doing all the laughing as I returned to the pits, the car none the worse for its grassing, while I pondered on one of motor racing's most important rules: Never relax your concentration until you are back in the paddock! Jack had not seen the drama: he had left earlier and at the time had been busy force-landing a plane in a snowstorm, to prove that things don't always go right, even in the best regulated circles!

*Tight through the chicane. Blunsden says, 'This is one of the points where the quick response of the Brabham steering showed up particularly well.'*

# THE BRABHAM JUNIOR

JACK BRABHAM and Ron Tauranac know a lot about motor racing. It is thus scarcely surprising that the Brabham Formula Junior car was a success right from the start. Nevertheless, after a full season of racing some improvements have suggested themselves. Of these, the removal of the rear brakes from their inboard location is the most radical.

Inboard brakes reduce unsprung weight but they have many disadvantages. By removing them to the hubs, the improvement in cooling rendered the same 9 ins. discs so much more powerful that it was necessary to increase the front disc size by ½ in. It is in making engine or gearbox changes possible, without disconnecting and subsequently bleeding the brakes, that the greatest benefit has been obtained.

The front of the chassis has been lowered a little and more movement has been given in bump to both the front and rear suspension. The multi-tubular frame has been stiffened up with tubular bracing of the scuttle, and the rear of the chassis is also more rigid than before. The front suspension employs short top and longer bottom wishbones, both tubular, with ball joint swivels and Triumph Herald stub axles, the top wishbones being adjustable. Both the anti-roll torsion bar and the rack and pinion steering gear, which is of Brabham manufacture, are ahead of the suspension parts but behind the radiator.

The rear suspension has two pairs of long tubular members pivoting well forward on the chassis. Lateral location is by adjustable straight tubular members above the half shafts and wishbones beneath, with their double ends pivoting on the light alloy hub carriers. The suspension is by inclined telescopic dampers and helical springs front and rear. The half shafts have Metalastic inboard joints, eliminating sliding splines.

A simpler water cooling circuit without a header tank eliminates the "swill pot". A new seating position allows a lower screen to be used and the appearance of the car is particularly attractive. The battery is enclosed and carried under the driver's knees, which is becoming the standard position among cars of this category. A light alloy fuel tank is carried amidships and embraces the rear of the driver's seat.

The magnesium wheels are attached by four studs and carry 4.50 × 13 ins. and 5.50 × 13 ins. tyres at front and rear respectively. The exhaust pipe is carried well out behind to give a sufficiently long tuned length.

A Holbay-Ford engine is normally fitted with two twin-choke Weber carburetters. A Cosworth engine may be used if desired. The 5-speed gearbox is of Volkswagen parentage and 16 different ratios are available. The short gear lever is on the right of the driver and operates the selectors through a tubular universally jointed shaft.

The wheelbase is 7 ft. 6 ins., front track 4 ft. 2 ins. and rear 4 ft. 1 in. The price, without engine, is £1,280.

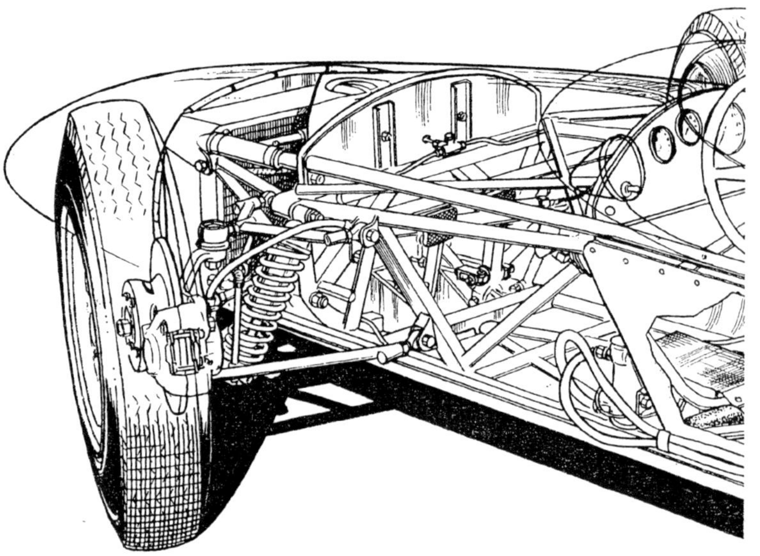

**REAR SUSPENSION** is shown in full detail

**FRONT SUSPENSION** incorporates adjustable top wishbones

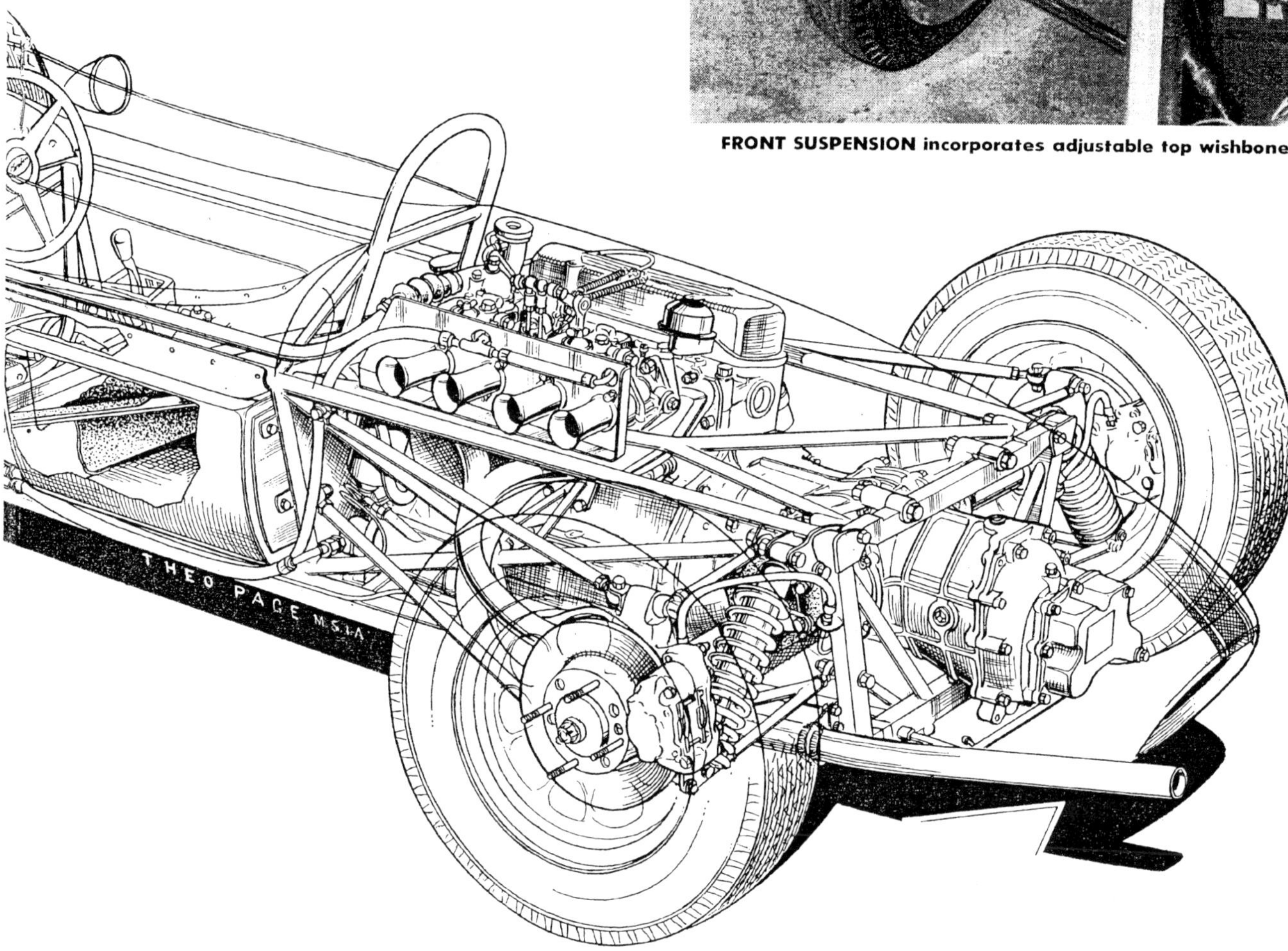


Jack Brabham's Formula Junior car for 1963 incorporates some improvements, the most radical of these being the change to outboard brakes at the rear. As well as a works-entered car, the Ian Walker Racing Team will be fielding two Juniors this year. Jack's Juniors should be well to the fore.

# JACK BRABHAM
## AND THE
# BRABHAM REPCO *BT 20*

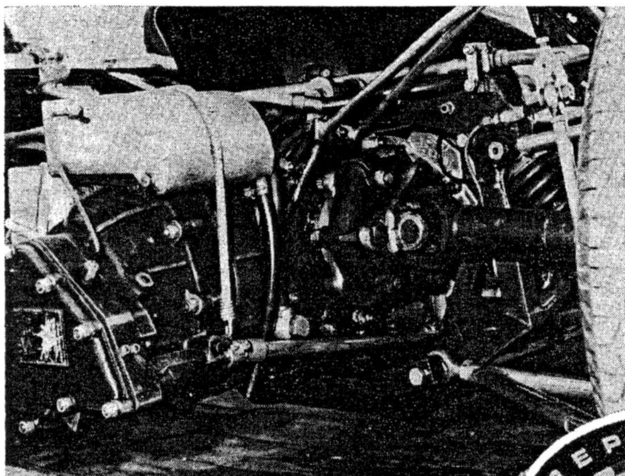

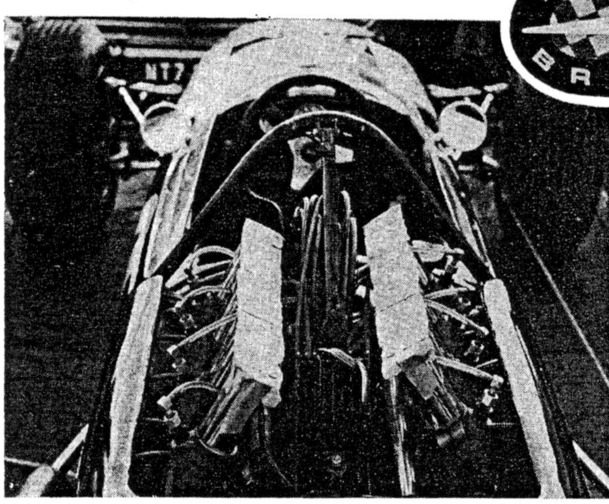

REAR suspension of the BT20 is by the now conventional single top link, reversed lower wishbone and twin radius arms, all rose-jointed for camber and toe-in adjustment. Clearly visible is the Hewland 5-speed gearbox, and the solid drive to the wheels, with rubber doughnuts being used to take up lateral movement.

FITTING snugly into the space frame, easily accessible, is the Repco V8 motor, based on an Oldsmobile motor produced by General Motors a few years ago. Note the "black box" between the fuel injection intakes which forms part of the transistorised ignition. The intakes are covered for travelling.

THE front suspension is by upper wishbones with the rear arm almost being a radius arm, while a lower, wide-based tubular wishbone is also used. An anti-roll bar is fitted, rose joints are fitted for camber adjustment and the front uprights are by Alford and Alder. The outboard Armstrong coil spring/damper unit can be seen.

NESTLED by the lower portion of the block is the alternator. Part of the exhaust system can also be seen, and various systems have been tried during the season, with increases in pipe bores being successful. To the extreme left of the photo the edge of the fuel tank can be seen.

# WORLD 1966 CHAMPIONS

**SIMPLICITY and lightness have formed the basis of the world championship drivers and constructors' winning Brabham Repco BT20, a car which few people rated as a good choice fcr the titles. But while the other marques may have been more powerful, they were also considerably heavier, more complicated and were thus less reliable.**

This year's Formula I car is the twentieth model from the Byfleet factory, the first being the MRD Formula Junior Brabham which was made in 1961. Since then a total of 250 Brabhams (including the sports cars) have been produced. Only two BT20s have been made, the second of which made its first appearance at the 1966 Italian G.P. for Denny Hulme to drive. Prior to this, the second of the works cars had been a BT19 (or the 1965 F.1 car fitted with a Repco motor).

Despite still being 150 lbs over the minimum weight limit, the Brabham was generally considered the lightest Formula I car during the 1966 season, and chief designer Ron Tauranac will be endeavouring to get the weight down on the 1967 machine. Because of the accessibility factor, Ron says that there is no intention of breaking away from the space frame construction. Additionally, accident repairs are both easier and cheaper, there is more design flexibility, and the car weighs no more than a monocque constructed car.

Round section tubing is used on the BT20, unlike the BT19 which had considerable oval tubing. The cockpit is double braced on the sides, and fuel is contained in aluminium pannier tanks which are attached to the chassis sides by straps with total capacity of 35 gallons. The frame itself weighs only 70 lbs or less than the F.3 Brabham chassis. Dimensions of the 1966 F.1 car are a little greater than the BT19 and the main figures are: wheelbase, 7ft. 9in.; front track, 4ft. 6½in.; rear track, 4ft. 6¾ in. Goodyear tyres have been used throughout the season.

These exclusive photos were taken by our Chief Photographer at Surfers Paradise in August.

Outboard mounted 11-inch Girling disc brakes are fitted all round and although 12-inch brakes were tried on Hulme's car for a few races, it was decided to revert to the smaller stoppers. Fifteen-inch wheels are fitted all round and the cast magnesium units have six-stud fixings.

The Repco motor has already been described previously, but basically the unit is a 90° V8 with a capacity of 2993 cc. Originally designed on an Oldsmobile motor, it is converted to single overhead camshafts with two valves per cylinder, Lucas fuel injection and Lucas transistorised ignition. Development in Britain and Australia has resulted in an output of 310 bhp at 7800 rpm, although the motor can be taken to 9000 rpm. A completely new motor is being produced for next season's F.1 car.

Four outright wins and a number of excellent placings have been the reward for the Brabham organisation in 1966. Two further models have been built — the BT21 (Formula 3 car for 1967) and the BT22, the Tasman cars which we will be seeing on New Zealand circuits next month.

**BRABHAM REPCO SUCCESSES, 1966**

**BELGIAN GRAND PRIX:**
Brabham fourth

**FRENCH GRAND PRIX:**
Brabham first Hulme third

**BRITISH GRAND PRIX:**
Brabham first Hulme Second

**DUTCH GRAND PRIX:**
Brabham first

**GERMAN GRAND PRIX:**
Brabham first

**ITALIAN GRAND PRIX:**
Hulme third

**MEXICAN GRAND PRIX:**
Brabham second Hulme third

**CHAMPIONSHIP PLACINGS**

J. **Brabham** (Brabham Repco), 1.
J. **Surtees** (Ferrari and Cooper), 2.
J. **Rindt** (Cooper Maserati), 3.
D. **Hulme** (Brabham Repco), 4.